TREASURE HOUSE

Teacher's Guide 4
Spelling Skills

Author: Sarah Snashall

HarperCollins
P U B L I S H E R S
200

William Collins' dream of knowledge for all began with the publication of his first book in 1819.

A self-educated mill worker, he not only enriched millions of lives, but also founded a flourishing publishing house. Today, staying true to this spirit, Collins books are packed with inspiration, innovation and practical expertise. They place you at the centre of a world of possibility and give you exactly what you need to explore it.

Collins. Freedom to teach.

Published by Collins
An imprint of HarperCollins*Publishers*
The News Building
1 London Bridge Street
London
SE1 9GF

Browse the complete Collins catalogue at
www.collins.co.uk

10 9 8 7 6 5 4 3 2 1

978-0-00-822311-3

British Library Cataloguing in Publication Data

A catalogue record for this publication is available from the British Library.

Publishing Director: Lee Newman
Publishing Manager: Helen Doran
Senior Editor: Hannah Dove
Project Manager: Emily Hooton
Author: Sarah Snashall
Development Editor: Jessica Marshall
Copy-editor: Karen Williams
Proofreader: Ros and Chris Davies
Cover design and artwork: Amparo Barrera and Ken Vail Graphic Design
Internal design concept: Amparo Barrera
Typesetter: Jouve India Private Ltd
Illustrations: Alberto Saichann (Beehive Illustration)
Production Controller: Rachel Weaver

Printed and bound by CPI Group (UK) Ltd, Croydon, CR0 4YY

Contents

About Treasure House

Treasure House is a comprehensive and flexible bank of books and online resources for teaching the English curriculum. The Treasure House series offers two different pathways: one covering each English strand discretely (Skills Focus Pathway) and one integrating texts and the strands to create a programme of study (Integrated English Pathway). This Teacher's Guide is part of the Skills Focus Pathway.

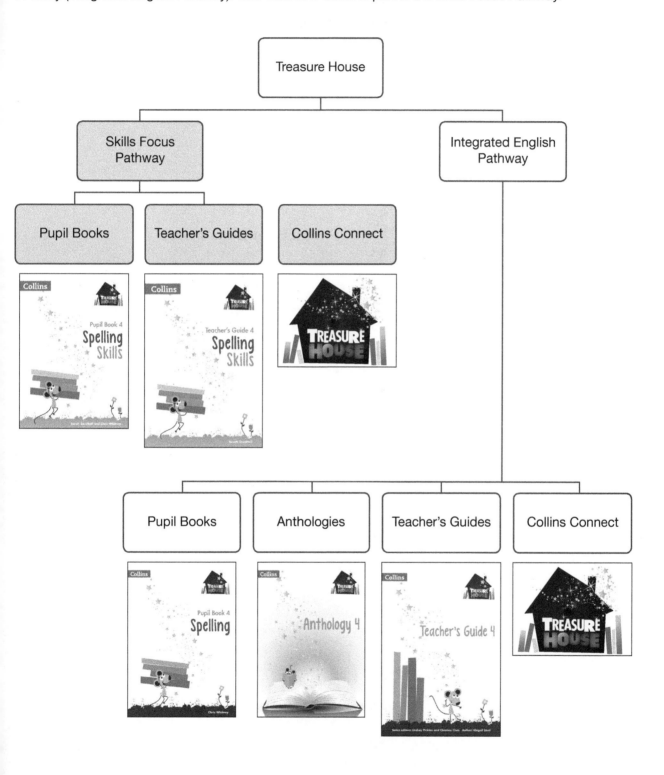

1. Skills Focus

The Skills Focus Pupil Books and Teacher's Guides for all four strands (Comprehension; Spelling; Composition; and Vocabulary, Grammar and Punctuation) allow you to teach each curriculum area in a targeted way. Each unit in the Pupil Book is mapped directly to the statutory requirements of the National Curriculum. Each Teacher's Guide provides step-by-step instructions to guide you through the Pupil Book activities and digital Collins Connect resources for each competency. With a clear focus on skills and clearly-listed curriculum objectives you can select the appropriate resources to support your lessons.

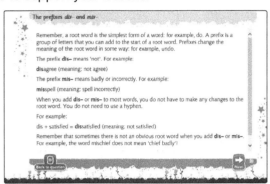

2. Integrated English

Alternatively, the Integrated English pathway offers a complete programme of genre-based teaching sequences. There is one Teacher's Guide and one Anthology for each year group. Each Teacher's Guide provides 15 teaching sequences focused on different genres of text such as fairy tales, letters and newspaper articles. The Anthologies contain the classic texts, fiction, non-fiction and poetry required for each sequence. Each sequence also weaves together all four dimensions of the National Curriculum for English – Comprehension; Spelling; Composition; and Vocabulary, Grammar and Punctuation – into a complete English programme. The Pupil Books and Collins Connect provide targeted explanation of key points and practice activities organised by strand. This programme provides 30 weeks of teaching inspiration.

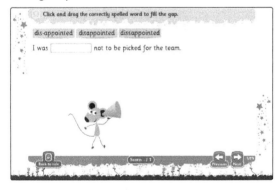

Other components

Handwriting Books, Handwriting Workbooks, Word Books and the online digital resources on Collins Connect are suitable for use with both pathways.

Treasure House Skills Focus Teacher's Guides

Year	Comprehension	Composition	Vocabulary, Grammar and Punctuation	Spelling
1	978-0-00-822290-1	978-0-00-822302-1	978-0-00-822296-3	978-0-00-822308-3
2	978-0-00-822291-8	978-0-00-822303-8	978-0-00-822297-0	978-0-00-822309-0
3	978-0-00-822292-5	978-0-00-822304-5	978-0-00-822298-7	978-0-00-822310-6
4	978-0-00-822293-2	978-0-00-822305-2	978-0-00-822299-4	978-0-00-822311-3
5	978-0-00-822294-9	978-0-00-822306-9	978-0-00-822300-7	978-0-00-822312-0
6	978-0-00-822295-6	978-0-00-822307-6	978-0-00-822301-4	978-0-00-822313-7

Inside the Skills Focus Teacher's Guides

The teaching notes in each unit of the Teacher's Guide provide you with subject information or background, a range of whole class and differentiated activities including photocopiable resource sheets and links to the Pupil Book and the online Collins Connect activities.

Each **Overview** provides clear objectives for each lesson tied into the new curriculum, links to the other relevant components and a list of any additional resources required.

Teaching overview introduces each spelling rule and provides a list of key words that follow the rule that are useful to the age group.

Support, embed & challenge supports a mastery approach with activities provided at three levels.

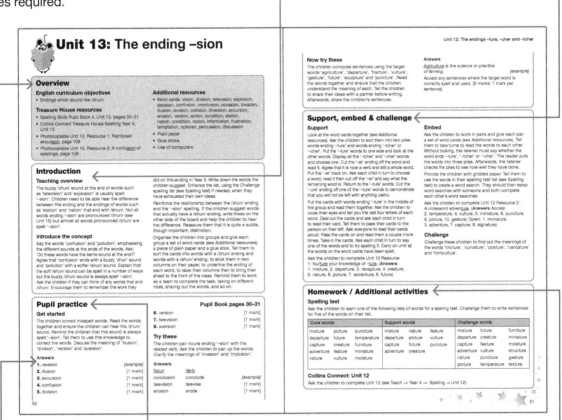

Introduce the concept provides 5–10 minutes of preliminary discussion points or class/group activities to get the pupils engaged in the lesson focus and set out any essential prior learning.

Pupil practice gives guidance and the answers to each of the three sections in the Pupil Book: *Get started*, *Try these* and *Now try these*.

Homework / Additional activities lists ideas for classroom or homework activities, and relevant activities from Collins Connect.

Two photocopiable **resource** worksheets per unit provide extra practice of the specific lesson concept. They are designed to be used with the activities in support, embed or challenge sections.

Treasure House Skills Focus Pupil Books

There are four Skills Focus Pupil Books for each year group, based on the four dimensions of the National Curriculum for English: Comprehension; Spelling; Composition; and Vocabulary, Grammar and Punctuation. The Pupil Books provide a child-friendly introduction to each subject and a range of initial activities for independent pupil-led learning. A Review unit for each term assesses pupils' progress.

Year	Comprehension	Composition	Vocabulary, Grammar and Punctuation	Spelling
1	978-0-00-823634-2	978-0-00-823646-5	978-0-00-823640-3	978-0-00-823652-6
2	978-0-00-823635-9	978-0-00-823647-2	978-0-00-823641-0	978-0-00-823653-3
3	978-0-00-823636-6	978-0-00-823648-9	978-0-00-823642-7	978-0-00-823654-0
4	978-0-00-823637-3	978-0-00-823649-6	978-0-00-823643-4	978-0-00-823655-7
5	978-0-00-823638-0	978-0-00-823650-2	978-0-00-823644-1	978-0-00-823656-4
6	978-0-00-823639-7	978-0-00-823651-9	978-0-00-823645-8	978-0-00-823657-1

Inside the Skills Focus Pupil Books

Comprehension

Includes high-quality text extracts covering poetry, prose, traditional tales, playscripts and non-fiction.

Pupils retrieve and record information, learn to draw inferences from texts and increase their familiarity with a wide range of literary genres.

Composition

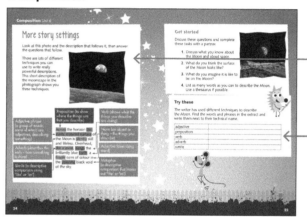

Includes high-quality, annotated text extracts as models for different types of writing.

Children learn how to write effectively and for a purpose.

Vocabulary, Grammar and Punctuation

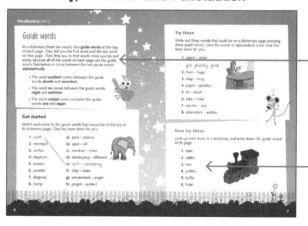

Develops children's knowledge and understanding of grammar and punctuation skills.

A rule is introduced and explained. Children are given lots of opportunities to practise using it.

Spelling

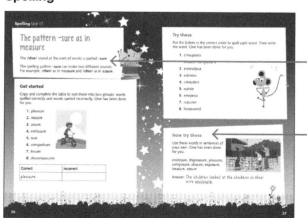

Spelling rules are introduced and explained.

Practice is provided for spotting and using the spelling rules, correcting misspelt words and using the words in context.

Treasure House on Collins Connect

Digital resources for Treasure House are available on Collins Connect which provides a wealth of interactive activities. Treasure House is organised into six core areas on Collins Connect:

- Comprehension
- Spelling
- Composition
- Vocabulary, Grammar and Punctuation
- The Reading Attic
- Teacher's Guides and Anthologies.

For most units in the Skills Focus Pupil Books, there is an accompanying Collins Connect unit focused on the same teaching objective. These fun, independent activities can be used for initial pupil-led learning, or for further practice using a different learning environment. Either way, with Collins Connect, you have a wealth of questions to help children embed their learning.

Treasure House on Collins Connect is available via subscription at connect.collins.co.uk

Features of Treasure House on Collins Connect

The digital resources enhance children's comprehension, spelling, composition, and vocabulary, grammar, punctuation skills through providing:

- a bank of varied and engaging interactive activities so children can practise their skills independently
- audio support to help children access the texts and activities
- auto-mark functionality so children receive instant feedback and have the opportunity to repeat tasks.

Teachers benefit from useful resources and time-saving tools including:

- teacher-facing materials such as audio and explanations for front-of-class teaching or pupil-led learning
- lesson starter videos for some Composition units
- downloadable teaching notes for all online activities
- downloadable teaching notes for Skills Focus and Integrated English pathways
- the option to assign homework activities to your classes
- class records to monitor progress.

Comprehension

- Includes high-quality text extracts covering poetry, prose, traditional tales, playscripts and non-fiction.
- Audio function supports children to access the text and the activities

Composition

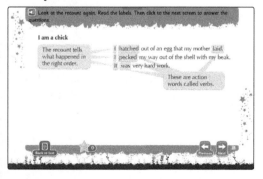

- Activities support children to develop and build more sophisticated sentence structures.
- Every unit ends with a longer piece of writing that can be submitted to the teacher for marking.

Vocabulary, Grammar and Punctuation

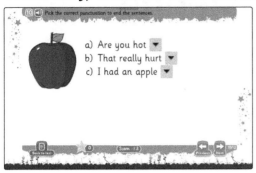

- Fun, practical activities develop children's knowledge and understanding of grammar and punctuation skills.
- Each skill is reinforced with a huge, varied bank of practice questions.

Spelling

- Fun, practical activities develop children's knowledge and understanding of each spelling rule.
- Each rule is reinforced with a huge, varied bank of practice questions.
- Children spell words using an audio prompt, write their own sentences and practise spelling using Look Say Cover Write Check.

Reading Attic

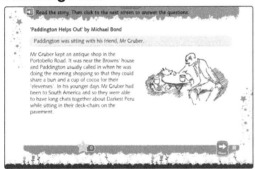

- Children's love of reading is nurtured with texts from exciting children's authors including Micheal Bond, David Walliams and Micheal Morpurgo.
- Lesson sequences accompany the texts, with drama opportunities and creative strategies for engaging children with key themes, characters and plots.
- Whole-book projects encourage reading for pleasure.

Treasure House Digital Teacher's Guides and Anthologies

The teaching sequences and anthology texts for each year group are included as a flexible bank of resources.

The teaching notes for each skill strand and year group are also included on Collins Connect.

Support, embed and challenge

Treasure House provides comprehensive, detailed differentiation at three levels to ensure that all children are able to access achievement. It is important that children master the basic skills before they go further in their learning. Children may make progress towards the standard at different speeds, with some not reaching it until the very end of the year.

In the Teacher's Guide, Support, Embed and Challenge sections allow teachers to keep the whole class focussed with no child left behind. Two photocopiable resources per unit offer additional material linked to the Support, Embed or Challenge sections.

Support

The Support section in Spelling offers scaffolded activities (suitable for use in small groups with adult support) that will help learners who have not yet grasped the specific spelling rule. These activities use fewer or more straightforward words and are usually supported with a photocopiable resource sheet.

If you have a teaching assistant, you may wish to ask him or her to help children work through these activities. You might then ask children who have completed these activities to progress to other more challenging tasks found in the Embed or Challenge sections – or you may decide more practice of the basics is required. Collins Connect can provide further activities.

Embed

The Embed section includes activities to embed learning and is aimed at those who children who are working at the expected standard. It ensures that learners have understood key teaching objectives for the age-group. These activities could be used by the whole class or groups, and most are appropriate for both teacher-led and independent work.

In Spelling, the Embed section provides activities to embed learning following the whole class introduction and is aimed at those who children who are working at the expected standard. After the children have learnt each rule, this section provides a range of fun small group games and activities to help the children (working without an adult) to learn words with the spelling pattern. A photocopiable resource sheet is provided for each unit.

Challenge

The Challenge section provides additional tasks, questions or activities that will push children who have mastered the spelling rule without difficulty. This keeps children motivated and allows them to gain a greater depth of understanding. You may wish to give these activities to fast finishers to work through independently.

Children who are working above the expected level may progress to focusing on the spelling of less common, longer words or they might investigate exceptions to the rule and creating posters for the class. Challenge activities are provided to stretch the children's understanding of the rule or to enhance vocabulary work.

Differentiated spelling lists

In the Homework section, you will find word lists for spelling tests. There is a standard list and there are also two targeted lists; *Support words* list is suitable for children who are struggling with the concept. The list is shorter and contains words that are more common, shorter, simpler or more regular. The *Challenge words* list is a longer list often with more challenging words, suitable for children who have grasped the rule/concept.

Differentiated weekly spelling lists are provided for each unit and details of any matching Collins Connect units.

Assessment

Teacher's Guide

There are opportunities for assessment throughout the Treasure House series. The teaching notes in the Skills Focus Teacher's Guides offer ideas for questions, informal assessment and spelling tests.

Pupil Book Review units

Each Pupil Book has three Review units designed as a quick formative assessment tool for the end of each term. Questions assess the work that has been covered over the previous units. These review units will provide you with an informal way of measuring your pupils' progress. You may wish to use these as Assessment *for* Learning to help you and your pupils to understand where they are in their learning journey.

The Review units in the Spelling and Vocabulary, Grammar and Punctuation Pupil Books, include questions testing rules taught in preceding units. By mixing questions on different unit topics within exercises, children can show understanding of multiple rules and patterns.

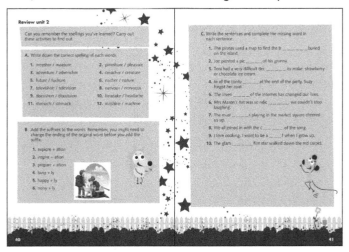

Assessment in Collins Connect

Activities on Collins Connect can also be used for effective assessment. Activities with auto-marking mean that if children answer incorrectly, they can make another attempt helping them to analyse their own work for mistakes. Homework activities can also be assigned to classes through Collins Connect. At the end of activities, children can select a smiley face to indicate how they found the task giving you useful feedback on any gaps in knowledge.

Class records on Collins Connect allow you to get an overview of children's progress with several features. You can choose to view records by unit, pupil or strand. By viewing detailed scores, you can view pupils' scores question by question in a clear table-format to help you establish areas where there might be particular strengths and weaknesses both class-wide and for individuals.

If you wish, you can also set mastery judgements (mastery achieved and exceeded, mastery achieved, mastery not yet achieved) to help see where your children need more help.

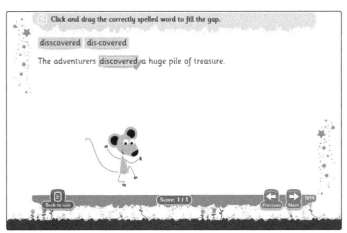

Support with teaching spelling

Trying to teach and understand the vagaries of English spelling is enough to drive the most patient of us to distraction. Think on those lucky countries such as Poland with phonetically consistent spelling. However, many words in English are phonetic and this should remain our starting point for all unknown words, with the children becoming increasingly confident in their knowledge of the spelling options for each sound.

The National Curriculum in England encourages us to teach the rules and patterns that are associated with each spelling cluster. In some cases these rules are easy to absorb, for example 'i before c except after c'. Others remain more elusive, such as hearing the stress in a word before deciding whether to double the last letter or not. You will have to judge for yourself when the rule is going to aid children in their learning and when they would be better off just learning the rules. (There are times when you have just got your head around a complicated rule to discover that there are only five suitable words for your class.) However, a knowledge and understanding of rules that do apply will provide children with the skills to manipulate language and root words, such as by adding suffixes and prefixes, to create specific vocabulary for their writing. This in turn will increase their confidence in writing. Teaching children to understand the relationship between words, such as 'grace' and 'gracious' not only develops their vocabulary but aids their spelling too.

This spelling scheme by its nature focuses on learning words as a separate activity: games, spelling tests and sometimes sentences. But, of course, this is only part of the picture. Children who read a lot will naturally absorb spelling as they regularly come across common words. Children who write a lot will naturally practise words that they want to use. Learning to spell words is only of any use if you use them at some point. Therefore, the activities in this scheme can only form part of the picture.

Weekly spelling test

The weekly spelling test remains crucial to learning the huge bank of words needed by the end of primary school. Spelling lists are provided in this scheme, but you may want to add or remove words depending on the abilities of the children in your class and the number of words you feel it is appropriate for them to learn. You will need to strike a balance between developing their vocabulary and providing useful words for them to learn.

You may also wish to enhance their spelling lists with words that they have spelt wrong during their writing tasks, or specific topic-led vocabulary.

Spelling games

The activities in this scheme aim to be fun and game-like. Many of the activities in the book are introduced for use with a particular set of words but many can be adapted for any word list you are practising (they mainly involve creating a set of word cards):

Pairs: Create two sets of word cards for the words you are practising and use them to play a game of pairs. Alternatively, use words with and without suffixes and prefixes or words related in other ways (such as different spellings for the same sound or homophones) and challenge the children to find the two associated words.

Simon's Game: When asking the children to learn a specific set of words, such as words with 'c' for /s/, ask pairs of children to remember the words on the list.

Pick a card: the children place a set of word cards between them and take turns to draw a card and test their partner or the next child around the table.

Hangman: Tell the children to play Hangman using words from previous two or three weeks' spellings. This encourages an attention to the specific letters and can be particularly useful when practising words with silent letters.

Bingo: Create Bingo cards for the words you are studying (ensuring each card has a slightly different word selection). When playing Bingo, the children spend the session staring at the words on their sheet – a useful way to add the word to the subconscious.

Game board: Create a simple board game where the children roll a dice to progress along a series of squares some of which require them to spell one of the words from the list (when someone draws a card and reads it to them). The board can be reused with any new set of words cards.

Differentiation

The lesson plans in this book provide three levels of differentiation. However, you may wish to provide further practice (Support or Challenge) at Years 3 and 4 or Years 5 and 6 by supplying the relevant children with the book for the other year group, as the words covered are the same. You may also wish to recap on words from earlier years for those children whose spelling needs further help.

meet	aircraft	plane	long hair
animal flesh	fair	mane	piece
fare	light fog	encounter	meat
calmness	plain	part of something	light or pleasant
failed to catch	most important	missed	peace
main	mist	cost of travel	obvious or basic

ate	prey	slay	way
sheikh	weight	rain	sleigh
veil	vein	eight	shake
vain	pray	reign	vale
weigh	wait	neigh	nay

Delivering the 2014 National Curriculum for English

Unit	Title	Treasure House resources	Collins Connect	English Programme of Study	KS2 English Grammar, Punctuation and Spelling Test code
1	Adding suffixes beginning with vowels to words of more than one syllable	• Spelling Skills Pupil Book 4, Unit 1, pages 4–5 • Spelling Skills Teacher's Guide 4 – Unit 1, pages 22–24 – Photocopiable Unit 1, Resource 1: To double or not to double, page 84 – Photocopiable Unit 1, Resource 2: Perfecting your spelling, page 85	Treasure House Spelling Year 4, Unit 1	Adding suffixes beginning with vowel letters to words of more than one syllable	S38 G6.3
2	The /i/ sound spelt y	• Spelling Skills Pupil Book 4, Unit 2, pages 6–7 • Spelling Skills Teacher's Guide 4 – Unit 2, pages 25–27 – Photocopiable Unit 2, Resource 1: Mysterious word search, page 86 – Photocopiable Unit 2, Resource 2: Crystal clear spellings, page 87	Treasure House Spelling Year 4, Unit 2	The /i/ sound spelt y elsewhere than at the end of words	S39
3	The /ʌ/ sound spelt ou	• Spelling Skills Pupil Book 4, Unit 3, pages 8–9 • Spelling Skills Teacher's Guide 4 – Unit 3, pages 28–29 – Photocopiable Unit 3, Resource 1: Eleanor and the dragon, page 88 – Photocopiable Unit 3, Resource 2: A rough, tough spelling game, page 89	Treasure House Spelling Year 4, Unit 3	The /ʌ/ sound spelt ou	S40
4	The prefixes dis– and mis–	• Spelling Skills Pupil Book 4, Unit 4, pages 10–11 • Spelling Skills Teacher's Guide 4 – Unit 4, pages 30–31 – Photocopiable Unit 4, Resource 1: Are they distakes or mistakes? page 90 – Photocopiable Unit 4, Resource 2: Choosing dis– or mis–, page 91	Treasure House Spelling Year 4, Unit 4	More prefixes	S41 G6.2

Unit	Title	Treasure House resources	Collins Connect	English Programme of Study	KS2 English Grammar, Punctuation and Spelling Test code

5	The prefixes in–, ir– im– and il–	• Spelling Skills Pupil Book 4, Unit 5, pages 12–13
		• Spelling Skills Teacher's Guide 4
		  – Unit 5, pages 32–34
		  – Photocopiable Unit 5, Resource 1: Incorrect or imcorrect: which is correct? page 92
		  – Photocopiable Unit 5, Resource 2: An incomplete crossword (to complete), page 93
			Treasure House Spelling Year 4, Unit 5	More prefixes	S41
					G6.2

6	The prefixes re– and inter–	• Spelling Skills Pupil Book 4, Unit 6, pages 14–15
		• Spelling Skills Teacher's Guide 4
		  – Unit 6, pages 35–36
		  – Photocopiable Unit 6, Resource 1: Interconnected meanings, page 94
		  – Photocopiable Unit 6, Resource 2: Prefix mix, page 95
			Treasure House Spelling Year 4, Unit 6	More prefixes	S41
					G6.2

7	The prefixes sub– and super–	• Spelling Skills Pupil Book 4, Unit 7, pages 16–17
		• Spelling Skills Teacher's Guide 4
		  – Unit 7, pages 37–38
		  – Photocopiable Unit 7, Resource 1: Super spellings, page 96
		  – Photocopiable Unit 7, Resource 2: Don't subscribe to substandard spelling! page 97
			Treasure House Spelling Year 4, Unit 7	More prefixes	S41
					G6.2

8	The prefixes anti– and auto–	• Spelling Skills Pupil Book 4, Unit 8, pages 18–19
		• Spelling Skills Teacher's Guide 4
		  – Unit 8, pages 39–41
		  – Photocopiable Unit 8, Resource 1: Automatically spell correctly, page 98
		  – Photocopiable Unit 8, Resource 2: Auto– or anti–? page 99
			Treasure House Spelling Year 4, Unit 8	More prefixes	S41
					G6.2

9	The suffix –ation	• Spelling Skills Pupil Book 4, Unit 9, pages 22–23
		• Spelling Skills Teacher's Guide 4
		  – Unit 9, pages 43–45
		  – Photocopiable Unit 9, Resource 1: An –ation examination, page 100
		  – Photocopiable Unit 9, Resource 2: Experimentation in adding –ation, page 101
			Treasure House Spelling Year 4, Unit 9	The suffix –ation	S42

Unit	Title	Treasure House resources	Collins Connect	English Programme of Study	KS2 English Grammar, Punctuation and Spelling Test code

10	The suffix –ly	• Spelling Skills Pupil Book 4, Unit 10, pages 24–25
		• Spelling Skills Teacher's Guide 4
		  – Unit 10, pages 46–47
		  – Photocopiable Unit 10, Resource 1: Adverb pairs, page 102
		  – Photocopiable Unit 10, Resource 2: Skilfully and capably spelling words ending –ly, page 103
			Treasure House Spelling Year 4, Unit 10	The suffix –ly	S43
					G6.3

11	The ending –sure	• Spelling Skills Pupil Book 4, Unit 11, pages 26–27
		• Spelling Skills Teacher's Guide 4
		  – Unit 11, pages 48–49
		  – Photocopiable Unit 11, Resource 1: Leisure bingo! page 104
		  – Photocopiable Unit 11, Resource 2: It's a pleasure spelling sure, page 105
			Treasure House Spelling Year 4, Unit 11	Words with endings sounding like /ʒə/ or /tʃə/	S44

12	The endings –ture, –cher and –tcher	• Spelling Skills Pupil Book 4, Unit 12, pages 28–29
		• Spelling Skills Teacher's Guide 4
		  – Unit 12, pages 50–51
		  – Photocopiable Unit 12, Resource 1: Nurture your knowledge of –ture, page 106
		  – Photocopiable Unit 12, Resource 2: A crossword adventure, page 107
			Treasure House Spelling Year 4, Unit 12	Words with endings sounding like /ʒə/ or /tʃə/	S44

13	The ending –sion	• Spelling Skills Pupil Book 4, Unit 13, pages 30–31
		• Spelling Skills Teacher's Guide 4
		  – Unit 13, pages 52–53
		  – Photocopiable Unit 13, Resource 1: Rainforest excursion, page 108
		  – Photocopiable Unit 13, Resource 2: A confusion of spellings, page 109
			Treasure House Spelling Year 4, Unit 13	Endings which sound like /ʒən/	S45

14	The suffix –ous	• Spelling Skills Pupil Book 4, Unit 14, pages 32–33
		• Spelling Skills Teacher's Guide 4
		  – Unit 14, pages 54–56
		  – Photocopiable Unit 14, Resource 1: Serious spellings, page 110
		  – Photocopiable Unit 14, Resource 2: Marvellous –ous words, page 111
			Treasure House Spelling Year 4, Unit 14	The suffix –ous	S46

Unit	Title	Treasure House resources	Collins Connect	English Programme of Study	KS2 English Grammar, Punctuation and Spelling Test code

15	The endings –tion, –sion, –ssion and –cian	• Spelling Skills Pupil Book 4, Unit 15, pages 34–35
		• Spelling Skills Teacher's Guide 4
		  – Unit 15, pages 57–59
		  – Photocopiable Unit 15, Resource 1: /shun/ collections, page 112
		  – Photocopiable Unit 15, Resource 2: Your mission: Learn these spellings, page 113
			Treasure House Spelling Year 4, Unit 15	Endings which sound like /ʃən/, spelt –tion, –sion, –ssion, –cian	S47

16	The /k/ sound spelt ch	• Spelling Skills Pupil Book 4, Unit 16, pages 36–37
		• Spelling Skills Teacher's Guide 4
		  – Unit 16, pages 60–61
		  – Photocopiable Unit 16, Resource 1: Spellings to make your head ache, page 114
		  – Photocopiable Unit 16, Resource 2: A schooling in /k/ spelt ch, page 115
			Treasure House Spelling Year 4, Unit 16	Words with the /k/ sound spelt ch (Greek in origin)	S48

17	The /sh/ sound spelt ch	• Spelling Skills Pupil Book 4, Unit 17, pages 38–39
		• Spelling Skills Teacher's Guide 4
		  – Unit 17, pages 62–64
		  – Photocopiable Unit 17, Resource 1: /sh/ spelt ch bingo, page 116
		  – Photocopiable Unit 17, Resource 2: A niche spelling pattern, page 117
			Treasure House Spelling Year 4, Unit 17	Words with the /ʃ/ sound spelt ch (mostly French in origin)	S50
					S49

18	The /k/ sound spelt –que and the /g/ sound spelt –gue	• Spelling Skills Pupil Book 4, Unit 18, pages 42–43
		• Spelling Skills Teacher's Guide 4
		  – Unit 18, pages 66–68
		  – Photocopiable Unit 18, Resource 1: Conquer these grotesque spellings, page 118
		  – Photocopiable Unit 18, Resource 2: A crossword of intrigue, page 119
			Treasure House Spelling Year 4, Unit 18	Words ending with the /g/ sound spelt –gue and the /k/ sound spelt –que (French in origin)	S50

19	The /s/ sound spelt sc	• Spelling Skills Pupil Book 4, Unit 19, pages 44–45
		• Spelling Skills Teacher's Guide 4
		  – Unit 19, pages 69–70
		  – Photocopiable Unit 19, Resource 1: Fascinating spellings, page 120
		  – Photocopiable Unit 19, Resource 2: Scenic spellings, page 121
			Treasure House Spelling Year 4, Unit 19	Words with the /s/ sound spelt sc (Latin in origin)	S51

Unit	Title	Treasure House resources	Collins Connect	English Programme of Study	KS2 English Grammar, Punctuation and Spelling Test code

20	The /ay/ sound spelt ei, eigh and ey	• Spelling Skills Pupil Book 4, Unit 20, pages 46–47
		• Spelling Skills Teacher's Guide 4
		  – Unit 20, pages 71–72
		  – Photocopiable Unit 20, Resource 1: /ay/ homophones, page 122
		  – Photocopiable Unit 20, Resource 2: Obey the spelling rules, page 123
			Treasure House Spelling Year 4, Unit 20	Words with the /eɪ/ sound spelt ei, eigh, or ey	S52

21	The possessive apostrophe with plural words	• Spelling Skills Pupil Book 4, Unit 21, pages 48–49
		• Spelling Skills Teacher's Guide 4
		  – Unit 21, pages 73–74
		  – Photocopiable Unit 21, Resource 1: Today's challenge, page 124
		  – Photocopiable Unit 21, Resource 2: Plural nouns and possessive apostrophes, page 125
			Treasure House Spelling Year 4, Unit 21	Possessive apostrophe with plural words	G5.8

22	Homophones and near-homophones (1)	• Spelling Skills Pupil Book 4, Unit 22, pages 50–51
		• Spelling Skills Teacher's Guide 4
		  – Unit 22, pages 75–76
		  – Photocopiable Unit 22, Resource 1: Whose pairs? page 126
		  – Photocopiable Unit 22, Resource 2: Whether to use 'weather' or 'whether', page 127
			Treasure House Spelling Year 4, Unit 22	Homophones and near-homophones	S61

23	Homophones and near-homophones (2)	• Spelling Skills Pupil Book 4, Unit 23, pages 52–53
		• Spelling Skills Teacher's Guide 4
		  – Unit 23, pages 77–78
		  – Photocopiable Unit 23, Resource 1: Throw here, not there!, page 128
		  – Photocopiable Unit 23, Resource 2: Great spelling practise! page 129
			Treasure House Spelling Year 4, Unit 23	Homophones and near-homophones	S61

24	Homophones and near-homophones (3)	• Spelling Skills Pupil Book 4, Unit 24, pages 54–55
		• Spelling Skills Teacher's Guide 4
		  – Unit 24, pages 79–80
		  – Photocopiable Unit 24, Resource 1: Play fair, page 130
		  – Photocopiable Unit 24, Resource 2: Have you missed these homophones? page 131
			Treasure House Spelling Year 4, Unit 24	Homophones and near-homophones	S61

Unit	Title	Treasure House resources	Collins Connect	English Programme of Study	KS2 English Grammar, Punctuation and Spelling Test code
25	Homophones and near-homophones (4)	• Spelling Skills Pupil Book 4, Unit 25, pages 56–57 • Spelling Skills Teacher's Guide 4 – Unit 25, pages 81–82 – Photocopiable Unit 25, Resource 1: Win the game: <u>reign</u> supreme! page 132 – Photocopiable Unit 25, Resource 2: Homophones to make you <u>bawl</u>, page 133	Treasure House Spelling Year 4, Unit 25	Homophones and near-homophones	S61

Unit 1: Adding suffixes beginning with vowels to words of more than one syllable

Overview

English curriculum objectives

- Adding suffixes beginning with vowel letters to words of more than one syllable

Treasure House resources

- Spelling Skills Pupil Book 4, Unit 1, pages 4–5
- Collins Connect Treasure House Spelling Year 4, Unit 1
- Photocopiable Unit 1, Resource 1: To double or not to double, page 84

- Photocopiable Unit 1, Resource 2: Perfecting your spelling, page 85

Additional resources

- Word cards: prefer, forgot, begin, upset, transfer, regret, forbid, occur, refer, travel, label, cancel, marvel, signal, quarrel, open, listen, water, target, bellow, shadow, borrow, enrol, limit, commit, admit, visit, answer, wonder, wander

Introduction

Teaching overview

When adding suffixes such as '–ing', '–ed', '–en' or '–er' to words of two syllables (or more) that end vowel consonant, we need to know whether or not to double the last letter.

If the last syllable of the root word is stressed or ends in the letter 'l', the last consonant is doubled, for example, 'begin' → 'beginning', 'travel' → 'traveller', 'forbid' → 'forbidden'.

If the last syllable of the root word is not stressed or ends with a 'w' or 'y', the last consonant is not doubled, for example, 'listen' → 'listened', 'allow' → 'allowed', 'enjoy' → 'enjoyed'.

Introduce the concept

Write the rules for adding suffixes to words of two syllables that end vowel consonant on the board.

1. The stress is on the last syllable: double the last letter.
2. The word ends in 'l': double the last letter.
3. The word ends in 'w': just add the suffix.
4. The last syllable is not stressed: just add the suffix.

Give each child one of the word cards (see Additional resources) and ask them to discuss with a partner which of the rules applies to their word. Tell the children who think their word needs the last letter doubled before the suffix to stand on the left of the room, and the other children on the right. Tell them all to hold up their words and look across the room. Tell the two groups to check each other's words, making sure they are all in the right place.

Tell the children to return to their seats. Ask them to add '–ing' to the word on their word card and hold it up. Ask volunteers to write their word on the board next to the rules that apply to their word.

Pupil practice

Pupil Book pages 4–5

Get started

The children sort words into two groups: words where the last letter is not doubled when a suffix is added and words where it is. Tell the children to read each word and decide which syllable is stressed before checking on the rule. After they have completed their table, tell them to read each column. The stress should be the same in all the words in each column: strong first syllables in the first column; strong second syllables in the second column.

Answers

Consonant not doubled with suffix		Consonant doubled with suffix	
garden	*[example]*	begin	[1 mark]
listen	[1 mark]	prefer	[1 mark]
water	[1 mark]	forget	[1 mark]
answer	[1 mark]		

Try these

The children add the suffixes '–ed' and '–ing' to root words. Remind the children to establish where the stress is in the root word in order to decide whether to double the consonant before adding the suffixes.

Answers

Root word	Add '–ed'		Add '–ing'	
wonder	*wondered*	*[example]*	wondering	[1 mark]
regret	regretted	[1 mark]	regretting	[1 mark]
prefer	preferred	[1 mark]	preferring	[1 mark]
offer	offered	[1 mark]	offering	[1 mark]

Now try these

The children add '–er', '–ed' or '–ing' to the words 'enrol', 'forbid', 'target', 'limit', 'commit', 'cancel', 'admit' and 'visit' and then use them in sentences. Tell the children to work out the correct spelling of the word they want to use before using it in a sentence. Point out that all the words can take '–ing' and '–ed' but that not many of them can take '–er'. Remind the children that, if a root word ends in 'l', the last letter is doubled whatever the syllable stress.

Answers

Jack wished he had <u>enrolled</u> for swimming lessons.   *[example]*

Accept sentences in which the spellings and contexts of the target words are correct. [16 marks: 1 mark per correctly spelt target word; 1 mark per correct context]

Support, embed & challenge

Support

Ask the children to complete Unit 1 Resource 1: To double or not to double. (**Answers** Consonant doubled: be<u>ginn</u>er, up<u>sett</u>ing, <u>cancell</u>ing, for<u>bidd</u>en, <u>travell</u>ed; Consonant not doubled: <u>visi</u>ting, <u>opener</u>, <u>listen</u>er, <u>limi</u>ting, <u>offer</u>ing; <u>wa</u>ter, for<u>got</u>, <u>listen</u>, en<u>rol</u>, <u>open</u>, ad<u>mit</u>, <u>offer</u>, pre<u>fer</u>, co<u>mmit</u>, o<u>ccur</u>)

Afterwards, discuss their answers and talk about the syllable stress rule. Pick out those words where the stress is useful. Use the words 'prefer' and 'offer' to demonstrate the syllable stress rule further.

Place the word cards in the centre of the table face down. Ask the children to take turns to draw a card and decide whether the last letter needs to be doubled before adding '–ing'. Ask everyone in the group to write the new word.

Embed

Organise the children into small groups. Provide each group with a set of word cards (see Additional resources). Ask the children to place the cards face down in front of them. Each child should take a turn to select a card, show it to the group and then choose a suffix for the rest of the group to add to the word. The other children in the group should write the word (with the suffix added) on their whiteboards. Encourage the children to check that everyone in the group has spelt the word correctly.

Ask the children to complete Unit 1 Resource 2: Perfec<u>ting</u> your spelling. Afterwards, quiz them about the words without a double consonant. Ask: 'How did you know to pick this option?' (**Answers** preferring, watered, regretting, listener, labelled, enrolled, visiting, committing, elbowed, admitted, opener, occurring, offering, travelled, upsetting, targeting, cancelling, limiting, beginner, narrowed)

Challenge

Provide these children with some word cards (see Additional resources). Ask them to work in pairs to decide which of the suffixes '–ing', '–ed' and/or '–er' can be added to each word and which cannot. Ask: 'What other endings could you add?'

Homework / Additional activities

Spelling test

Ask the children to learn one of the following lists of words for a spelling test. Challenge them to write sentences for five of the words on their list.

Core words		Support words		Challenge words	
preferred	opened	beginning	opened	preferred	cancelled
beginning	listened	upsetting	listened	forgotten	admitting
upsetting	targeted	forbidden	limited	beginning	occurred
forbidden	limited	travelling	visited	upsetting	offered
occurred	visited	cancelled	offered	regretted	opened
travelling	wondering			forbidden	listened
cancelled	offered			travelling	watering
focussing				labelling	targeted
				focussing	limited
				committed	visited

Collins Connect: Unit 1

Ask the children to complete Unit 1 (see Teach → Year 4 → Spelling → Unit 1).

Unit 2: The /i/ sound spelt y

Overview

English curriculum objectives

- The /i/ sound spelt y elsewhere than at the end of words

Treasure House resources

- Spelling Skills Pupil Book 4, Unit 2, pages 6–7
- Collins Connect Treasure House Spelling Year 4, Unit 2
- Photocopiable Unit 2, Resource 1: Mysterious word search, page 86
- Photocopiable Unit 2, Resource 2: Crystal clear spellings, page 87

Additional resources

- Word cards: gym, myth, syrup, Egypt, crystal, pyramids, oxygen, typical, bicycle, mystery, symptoms, physics, symbol, system, Sydney, lynx, cymbal, abysmal, abyss, hysterical, lyrics
- Dice

Introduction

Teaching overview

There are about 20 words that are useful to Year 4 children that spell the short /i/ sound with the letter 'y'. There is no pattern. The words just need to be learned.

Introduce the concept

Write the words 'myth', 'syrup' and 'Egypt' on the board and ask the children to tell you what they need to remember about these words. Agree that it is the 'y' spelling for the /i/ sound. Organise the children into groups (ensuring there are a mix of abilities in each group). Challenge the groups to list as many other words with this spelling that they can think of. Encourage them to remember the work they did in Year 3 on this spelling pattern. Share their lists, awarding points if you feel it is appropriate: one for each correct word and a bonus point for each unique word. Compile a master list on the board. Give the children clues for any words they have not thought of yet, for example: 'a shiny stone with many sides' ('crystal'), 'a form of transport with two wheels, handlebars and pedals' ('bicycle'), 'another word for usual' ('typical'), 'the capital of Australia' ('Sydney').

Pupil practice

Pupil Book pages 6–7

Get started

The children copy and complete words by adding the missing letter, 'i' or 'y'. Afterwards, read the words together.

Answers

1. p_y_ramid	[example]
2. s_i_lly	[1 mark]
3. g_y_m	[1 mark]
4. cr_y_stal	[1 mark]
5. s_y_mptom	[1 mark]
6. pr_i_nce	[1 mark]
7. m_y_stery	[1 mark]
8. thr_i_lling	[1 mark]

Try these

The children decide whether the underlined words in each sentence are spelt correctly or not. They then write out the sentences, correcting and underlining the word that was misspelt.

Answers

1. *Nayati enjoyed visiting the* <u>pyramids</u> *and would remember them forever.*   [example]
2. The photos were amazing – now I want to go to <u>Egypt</u> too!   [1 mark]
3. This rainy weather is <u>typical</u> in winter!   [1 mark]
4. The music club's <u>symbol</u> is a violin.   [1 mark]
5. My Uncle Jim tells some very <u>mysterious</u> stories!   [1 mark]
6. The fluffy young <u>cygnets</u> will turn into elegant swans.   [1 mark]
7. Frankie had learned the <u>lyrics</u> to his favourite song.   [1 mark]
8. The <u>gymnast</u> did a flip and landed on her feet.   [1 mark]

Now try these

The children correct the spellings of words and use each corrected word in a sentence.

Answers

1. *Claire loves to play exciting <u>rhythms</u> on the drums.* *[example]*
2. syllable [1 mark]
3. physical [1 mark]

4. cymbal [1 mark]
5. hysterical [1 mark]
6. system [1 mark]
7. oxygen [1 mark]
8. lyric [1 mark]

Accept any sentence that uses the target word correctly. [7 marks: 1 mark per sentence]

Support, embed & challenge

Support

Read through the word cards with this group (see Additional resources). Focus on the words that are most useful and familiar: 'gym', 'myth', 'syrup', 'Egypt', 'crystal', 'pyramids', 'mystery', 'typical'. Give each child in the group one of the cards and ask them to become the expert in that word. Ask the children to take turns to roll a dice. When they throw a 1 or a 2, they must spell the word on their own card. When they throw a 3 or a 4, they can ask another member of the group to spell the word on the card that group member has. When they throw a 5 or 6, they can ask any person in the group to spell the word they have on their own card.

Ask the children to complete Unit 2 Resource 1: Mysterious word search.

Answers

a	c	g	g	k	s	y	r	u	p
e	E	g	y	p	t	f	h	d	b
k	p	h	m	h	d	m	k	f	i
m	y	s	t	e	r	y	a	q	c
f	r	y	e	c	q	t	t	x	y
d	a	m	b	j	x	h	z	h	c
q	m	b	c	r	y	s	t	a	l
b	i	o	c	e	j	f	a	d	e
f	d	l	s	y	s	t	e	m	g

Embed

Ask the children to play 'Hangman' with a partner, using only words with the /i/ sound spelt 'y'. Tell the children to come to you for a word, or to check their spelling, should they need to.

Write the words 'myth', 'symbol', 'crystal', 'Egypt', 'pyramids' and 'mystery' on the board. Tell them to work in groups to make up a story using the words. Explain that they can write their story as notes, as a story map, as a story board or write it out in full. Have the children present their stories to the class.

Ask the children to complete Unit 2 Resource 2: Crystal clear spellings. Explain that all the missing words have the /i/ sound spelt 'y'. (**Answers** 1. gym, 2. myth, 3. syrup, 4. pyramids, 5. crystals, 6. Egypt, 7. bicycles, 8. mystery)

Challenge

Provide these children with a longer, more challenging list of words to use in a more developed, polished story, for example, 'myth', 'symbol', 'crystal', 'Egypt', 'pyramids', 'mystery', 'abyss' and 'abysmal'.

Homework / Additional activities

Spelling test

Ask the children to learn one of the following lists of words for a spelling test. Challenge them to write sentences for five of the words on their list.

Core words		Support words		Challenge words	
gym	typical	gym	system	gym	mystery
myth	bicycle	myth	crystal	myth	lynx
syrup	mystery	syrup	pyramid	syrup	cymbal
Egypt	lynx	Egypt	bicycle	Egypt	abysmal
symbol	cymbal	symbol	mystery	symbol	symptom
system	abysmal			system	abyss
crystal	symptom			crystal	Sydney
pyramid				pyramid	hysterical
				typical	lyrics
				bicycle	

Collins Connect: Unit 2

Ask the children to complete Unit 2 (see Teach → Year 4 → Spelling → Unit 2).

# Unit 3: The /u/ sound spelt ou

Overview

English curriculum objectives
- The /u/ sound spelt ou

Treasure House resources
- Spelling Skills Pupil Book 4, Unit 3, pages 8–9
- Collins Connect Treasure House Spelling Year 4, Unit 3

- Photocopiable Unit 3, Resource 1: Eleanor and the dragon, page 88
- Photocopiable Unit 3, Resource 2: A rough, tough spelling game, page 89

Additional resources
- Counters (for Resource 2)

Introduction

Teaching overview

The short /u/ sound is spelt 'ou' in a number of common and useful words: 'trouble', 'double', 'couple', 'young', 'cousin', 'touch', 'courage', 'rough', 'tough', 'country', 'enough', 'flourish' and 'nourish'. Three of these, 'rough', 'tough' and 'enough', have the added complication of the /f/ sound spelt 'gh'.

Introduce the concept

Write the letters 'ou' on the board and ask the children what sound these letters represent. Provide examples of the different sounds they represent, such as 'loud', 'would' and 'soup'.

Write the words 'young' and 'cousin' on the board and ask the children to guess what the spelling focus will to be. Agree that it is the /u/ sound spelt 'ou'.

Challenge the children to think of as many words with this spelling as they can. Encourage them to remember the work they did in Year 3 on this spelling pattern. On the board, write words the children suggest, such as 'trouble', 'double', 'couple', 'young', 'cousin', 'touch', 'courage', 'country', 'rough', 'tough', 'enough', 'flourish', 'nourish'. Remind the children of any words they have forgotten.

Organise the children into groups and challenge each group to create a silly sentence using as many of the words as possible (whilst still making some sense). Share the sentences and award praise according to the number of words used and the quality of the sentence.

Discuss the meanings of 'flourish', 'nourish', 'flourishing' and 'nourishing'.

Pupil practice

Pupil Book pages 8–9

Get started

The children check the spellings of underlined words in sentences. Warn them that the words are a mixture of 'u' and 'ou' spellings. Afterwards, agree on the correct spellings.

Answers

1. *correct*			[example]
2. incorrect	[1 mark]	cousin	[1 mark]
3. correct			[1 mark]
4. incorrect	[1 mark]	trumpet	[1 mark]
5. correct			[1 mark]
6. correct			[1 mark]
7. incorrect	[1 mark]	hairbrush	[1 mark]
8. incorrect	[1 mark]	tough	[1 mark]

Try these

The children copy sentences, correcting the incorrectly spelt word in each sentence as they do so.

Encourage the children to identify the misspelt words before writing the sentences. Tell them to look out for words spelt with 'u' that should be spelt 'ou'.

Answers

1. *Grandad hasn't planted <u>enough</u> tomatoes.*

   [example]

2. Are you sure you have <u>enough</u> time to clean up before Mum comes back? [1 mark]

3. Mr Godwin always <u>encourages</u> us to enjoy science. [1 mark]

4. Rajesh saw a <u>couple</u> of robins nesting in the tree. [1 mark]

5. Kerry has a lot of <u>trouble</u> learning her spellings. [1 mark]

6. It's <u>tough</u> work climbing hills! [1 mark]

7. Zahra's cookery teacher said it was important to be well <u>nourished</u>. [1 mark]

8. You can look at the paintings but you can't <u>touch</u> them. [1 mark]

Now try these

The children correct the spellings of words and then use them in sentences.

Answers

1. *Katja finished her painting with a flourish. [example]*

2. couple   [1 mark]

3. nourish   [1 mark]

4. courage   [1 mark]

5. cousin   [1 mark]

6. double   [1 mark]

7. rough   [1 mark]

8. enough   [1 mark]

Accept any sentence that uses the target word correctly. [7 marks: 1 mark per sentence]

Support, embed & challenge

Support

Read the story on Unit 3 Resource 1: Eleanor and the dragon, with the children. Ask them to find the words in the story with the /u/ sound spelt 'ou'. (**Answers** cousins, young, trouble, enough, enough, tough, enough, country, rough, cousins, encourage, nourish, couple, cousins', courage, flourish)

Afterwards, write the words they have found in the first column of a chart, labelling the column /u/ spelt 'ou'. Find the words in the story with the /u/ sound spelt 'u' ('up', 'trudged', 'crushed' and 'swung'), /oo/ spelt 'ou' ('soups' and 'you're') and /ou/ spelt 'ou' ('foul', 'out', 'our', 'shouted' and 'about'). Create a column for each spelling pattern.

Cut out the words 'trouble', 'double', 'young', 'cousin', 'courage', 'rough', 'tough', 'flourish', 'enough', 'nourish', 'couple', 'country' and 'touch' from the game board on Unit 3 Resource 2: A r**ou**gh, t**ou**gh spelling game, and hold the words in your hand. You will also need a small pile of counters. Ask the children to recall the words with /u/ spelt 'ou'.

As the children volunteer each word, hand them the slip of paper with that word on as a prize. If they think of a word with /u/ spelt 'ou' that is not on Unit 3 Resource 2, hand them a counter, which is worth double points.

Embed

Ask the children to work in pairs and provide each pair with a copy of Unit 3 Resource 2: A r**ou**gh, t**ou**gh spelling game, and a counter. Tell them to take turns to throw the counter, close their eyes and spell the word they have landed on.

Tell the children to compose sentences for 'flourish' and 'nourish'.

Challenge

Challenge these children to write their own story using as many of the words from the Challenge spelling list as possible (see Spelling test).

Challenge them to, at some point during the week, use either 'flourish' or 'nourish' in a piece of writing that is not related to learning spellings.

Homework / Additional activities

Spelling test

Ask the children to learn one of the following lists of words for a spelling test. Challenge them to write sentences for five of the words on their list.

Core words		Support words		Challenge words	
trouble	rough	trouble	cousin	trouble	enough
double	tough	double	touch	double	flourish
couple	enough	couple	rough	couple	nourish
young	flourish	young	courage	young	encourage
cousin	nourish			cousin	country
touch	encourage			touch	encouraging
courage	country			courage	discourage
				rough	nourishing
				tough	

Collins Connect: Unit 3

Ask the children to complete Unit 3 (see Teach → Year 4 → Spelling → Unit 3).

Unit 4: The prefixes dis– and mis–

Introduction

Teaching overview

The prefixes 'dis–' and 'mis–' mean 'not', 'against' or other negations of the root word. Most words take one or the other, for example, 'disbelieve' rather than 'misbelieve', 'mistake' rather than 'distake'. Learning which prefix a root word takes is one of the main challenges for Year 4 children. When the prefix 'mis–' or 'dis–' is added to a root word, there is no change to the word, for example, 'dis' + 'cover' → 'discover', 'mis' + 'spell' → 'misspell'. However, there are many words where the original root word is either very obscure or has fallen out of use, for example, 'disgust'.

Introduce the concept

Write the words 'mistreat' and 'disorder' on the board and discuss their meanings. Ask: 'What are these words made up of?' Challenge the children to split the words into prefix and root. Ask: 'How do the prefixes 'dis–' and 'mis–' change words?' Ask the children to work in groups to compile lists of words starting with each prefix. Encourage the children to remember the work they did on these suffixes in Year 3. Inform the children that there are many more words that take the prefix 'dis–' than take 'mis–'. Share the lists of words. Discuss any uncommon words the children have thought of and any words where the root starts 's' (resulting in 'ss'), such as 'dissimilar'.

Pupil practice

Pupil Book pages 10–11

Get started

The children look at pairs of words and copy out the word from each pair that has the correct prefix. Before they do so, ask the children to read the words. Explain that only one of each pair is an actual word. Tell them to decide which one is correct.

Answers
1. *mismatched* [example]
2. disagree [1 mark]
3. misspell [1 mark]
4. misshape [1 mark]
5. discourage [1 mark]
6. disobey [1 mark]
7. misbehave [1 mark]
8. disgraceful [1 mark]

Try these

The children add the correct prefix, 'dis–' or 'mis–', to root words. Tell them to say the options aloud and decide which sounds right.

Answers
1. *misconduct* [example]
2. dishonest [1 mark]
3. disapproval [1 mark]
4. misguided [1 mark]
5. disconnect [1 mark]
6. misjudge [1 mark]
7. misunderstand [1 mark]
8. dislike [1 mark]

Now try these

The children add the correct prefix, 'dis–' or 'mis–', to root words and then use the words in sentences.

Answers

1. *Although they are twins, the girls' tastes are <u>dissimilar</u>.* [example]
2. disagree [1 mark]
3. mismatched [1 mark]
4. miscalculated [1 mark]
5. misjudge [1 mark]
6. dissatisfied [1 mark]
7. misunderstood [1 mark]
8. disloyal [1 mark]

Accept any sentence that uses the target word correctly. [7 marks: 1 mark per sentence]

Support, embed & challenge

Support

Use the word cards with these children (see Additional resources) to try out both prefixes on each root word. Allow time for the children to read the different words, and then choose the correct one. Clarify the meaning of each word, linking it to the meaning of the root word. Scribe the words for the children, pointing out how the spelling of the root word stays the same.

Demonstrate adding 'dis–' to 'similar' and 'mis–' to 'spell'. Ask them to point out the double 's' in the middle of the new words.

Ask the children to complete Unit 4 Resource 1: Are they <u>dis</u>takes or <u>mis</u>takes? (**Answers** mistaken, dislike, misunderstand, dishonest, disappear, mistake, disabled, misfortune, discomfort, mishap, disobey, disrupt)

Embed

Ask the children to complete Unit 4 Resource 2: Choosing <u>dis</u>– or <u>mis</u>–. Afterwards, discuss the answers and talk about the difference between 'displace' and 'misplace', 'disused' and 'misused' and 'discount' and 'miscount'. (**Answers** 1. discount, 2. miscount, 3. disused, 4. misused, 5. displaced, 6. misplaced, 7. misfortune, 8. discontinue, 9. dishonest, 10. misleading)

Ask the children to add 'dis–' to 'similar', 'satisfied' and 'service' and 'mis–' to 'spell', 'shapen', 'start', 'speak' and 'said'. Ask: 'What double letter will you end up with in the middle of each word?', 'Why will that happen?'

Organise the children into small groups and give each group a set of the word cards (see Additional resources). Ask them to spend time adding 'dis–' and 'mis–' to the words, deciding which prefix creates a real word and what each word means.

Challenge

Challenge these children to predict the meanings of the words 'misjudge', 'misdeed', 'disinfect' and 'distaste'. Have them look the words up in a dictionary to check their predictions.

Homework / Additional activities

Spelling test

Ask the children to learn one of the following lists of words for a spelling test. Challenge them to write sentences for five of the words on their list.

Core words		Support words		Challenge words	
disagree	dissimilar	disagree	misspell	disagree	distrust
disappear	misspell	disappear	mistaken	disappear	dismantle
discover	mistaken	discover	misplace	discover	misspell
dislike	misplace	dislike	misbehave	dislike	mistaken
dishonest	misbehave	disobey	misfortune	dishonest	misplace
disobey	misfortune			disobey	misbehave
disadvantage	mislaid			disadvantage	misfortune
disappointed				disappointed	mislaid
				dissimilar	misleading
				displace	misshapen

Collins Connect: Unit 4

Ask the children to complete Unit 4 (see Teach → Year 4 → Spelling → Unit 4).

Unit 5: The prefixes in–, ir–, im– and il–

Introduction

Teaching overview

The prefixes 'in–', 'il–' and 'ir–' are a difficult subject for Year 4 children, even though they will know many of the words already and will have learned about these prefixes in Year 3. The prefix 'in–' can mean 'un–' or it can mean an intensification of the original word. The negative connotation is more common. To make matters worse, depending on the root word, the spelling of 'in–' changes to 'il–', 'ir–' or 'im–'.

Introduce the concept

Write the words 'dependent', 'possible', 'legal' and 'responsible' on the board. Ask the children to discuss in their groups what the opposite of these words are. Agree that they are 'independent', 'impossible', 'illegal' and 'irresponsible'. Ask

volunteers to explain what the prefixes 'in–', 'im–', il–' and 'ir–' do to words and when to use which prefix. Encourage the children to remember the work they did on these prefixes in Year 3. Clarify that the prefixes 'in–', 'im–', 'il–' and 'ir–' are all versions of the same prefix, which changes depending on the spelling of the root word: root words beginning 'm' and 'p' take 'im–'; root words beginning 'l' take 'il–'; root words beginning 'r' take 'ir–'; all other root words take 'in–'.

Organise the children into groups. Write the words 'legal', 'logical', 'mature', 'mobile', 'patient', 'possible', 'practical', 'mortal', 'correct', 'credible', 'accurate', 'experienced', 'responsible' and 'regular' on the board. Ask the children to add the correct prefix to each word to create words that have opposite meanings to those of the root words.

Pupil practice

Pupil Book pages 12–13

Get started

The children separate words with prefixes into prefix and root. Afterwards, discuss which prefixes have been used with which words. Talk about the words with double letters.

Answers

1. ir / resistible	[example]
2. in / dependent	[1 mark]
3. in / definitely	[1 mark]
4. ir / replaceable	[1 mark]
5. il / legal	[1 mark]
6. ir / regular	[1 mark]
7. im / mortal	[1 mark]
8. in / correct	[1 mark]

Try these

The children copy and complete words by adding the correct prefix. Recap on the rules for choosing between these prefixes. Remind them that the prefix often matches the start of the root word (and 'im–' also goes with words beginning 'p'). If there is not a match, use 'in–'.

Answers

1. incredible	[example]
2. inconsiderate	[1 mark]
3. irresistible	[1 mark]
4. immobile	[1 mark]
5. inability	[1 mark]
6. illiterate	[1 mark]
7. impractical	[1 mark]
8. indescribable	[1 mark]

Now try these

The children compose sentences using the target words 'improbable', 'immeasurable', 'irreplaceable', 'independent', 'inability', 'illegible', 'immobile' and 'inescapable'. Read the words together and discuss the meaning of each. Ask the children to predict the meanings of words they are not sure about, using the meanings of the prefix and of the root as clues.

Answers

It is <u>improbable</u> that you will see a monkey riding on a crocodile.   *[example]*

Accept sentences where the target word is spelt correctly and the context is correct.
[8 marks: 1 mark per sentence]

Support, embed & challenge

Support

Display the word cards to the group (see Additional resources). Discuss the meaning of each root word. Recap the rules for adding these prefixes and then ask the children to sort the root words into those starting with 'm' or 'p', those starting 'r', those starting 'l' and then the rest. Provide the children with the prefix cards. Help them to add the correct prefix to each word and, together, read the root word and then the word with the prefix. Discuss the meaning of each word. Muddle up the root words and challenge the children to choose a root word and prefix to create a new word. Write the words, emphasising the correct choice of suffix.

Ask the children to complete Unit 5 Resource 1: Incorrect or imcorrect: which is correct? Read through the rules for adding the correct prefix at the top of the sheet with them beforehand. (**Answers** impossible, irrelevant, incorrect, illegal, immature, inactive, improper, inexact, imprison, incredible, impatient, irresponsible; competent, mortal, regular, legible)

Embed

Ask the children to complete Unit 5 Resource 2: An <u>in</u>complete crossword to complete. (**Answers** Across:

1. impatient, 3. imprison, 6. impossible, 7. illegal; Down: 2. incredible, 3. immortal, 4. immature, 5. illegible)

Ask the children to work in pairs to write opposite versions of these sentences.

'Tina's brother was mature, considerate, responsible and independent.'

'Sonja is a very practical person and found the DIY task possible.'

'Fergus was literate and had legible handwriting but told dreadful stories.'

Ask the children to work in pairs and provide each pair with a set of word cards (see Additional resources). Tell them to put the cards face down between them and take turns to turn over a card. Tell them to race each other to be the first to say the correct antonym by correctly adding 'in–', 'im–', 'ir–' or 'il–'.

Challenge

Ask these children to discuss the words 'inflame', 'imprison', 'import', 'immigrate', 'imperil' and 'inscribe' with a partner. Point out that the 'in–' or 'im–' prefix does not mean 'not' in these words. Ask them what they think it means.

Homework / Additional activities

Spelling test

Ask the children to learn one of the following lists of words for a spelling test. Challenge them to write sentences for five of the words on their list.

Core words		Support words		Challenge words	
incorrect	immortal	incorrect	impossible	incorrect	improper
incredible	impatient	incredible	imprison	incredible	immortal
inactive	imprison	inactive	irregular	inactive	impatient
inexact	irregular	incompetent	irresistible	inexact	imprison
incompetent	irresponsible	immature	irresponsible	inadequate	irregular
immature	irrelevant			insufficient	irresponsible
impossible	illegal			incompetent	irrelevant
improper				inconvenient	irresistible
				immature	illegal
				impossible	illegible

Collins Connect: Unit 5

Ask the children to complete Unit 5 (see Teach → Year 4 → Spelling → Unit 5).

Unit 6: The prefixes re– and inter–

Overview

English curriculum objectives
- More prefixes

Treasure House resources
- Spelling Skills Pupil Book 4, Unit 6, pages 14–15
- Collins Connect Treasure House Spelling Year 4, Unit 6
- Photocopiable Unit 6, Resource 1: Interconnected meanings, page 94

- Photocopiable Unit 6, Resource 2: Prefix mix, page 95

Additional resources
- Word cards: re– (multiple copies), inter– (multiple copies), place, plant, play, read, search, shape, tell, think, view, vision, cover, mix, paint, form, think, organise, city, com, net, act, national, change
- Dictionaries

Introduction

Teaching overview

The prefix 're–' means 'again'; the prefix 'inter–' means 'between'. As with previous prefixes, the root word does not change. There are many more commonly used words that begin 're–' than begin 'inter–'.

Introduce the concept

Mime tying your shoe laces then write 'I tied my shoe laces' on the board. Pretend they have come undone again and pretend to tie them again. Ask: 'What sentence could I write now?' Suggest 'I retied my shoe laces.' Ask: 'What has changed here?' Agree that 're–' has been added to 'tied' to give the

meaning 'again'. Write the words 'wrote', 'read', 'sew', 'heated', 'packed', 'planted' and 'considered' on the board. Ask volunteers to tell you the word with the 're–' prefix added. Ask other volunteers to tell you what each new word means, for example, 'wrote again', 'read again', 'sew again'. Ask the children what has happened to each root word. (It has remained unchanged.)

Write 'internet' on the board. Ask: 'What is this word made up of?' Agree it is the prefix 'inter–' plus the word 'net'. Ask the children to suggest words with the prefix 'inter–', such as 'international', 'interfere', 'interact' and 'intercity'. Encourage them to remember the work they did on these prefixes in Year 3.

Pupil practice

Pupil Book pages 14–15

Get started

The children add the prefix 're–' or 'inter–' to root words. Ask the children to try each prefix on the root word before choosing the correct one. Afterwards, discuss the meanings of the new words.

Answers
1. *reroute*   *[example]*
2. interdepartmental   [1 mark]
3. reinterpret   [1 mark]
4. recall   [1 mark]
5. reconsider   [1 mark]
6. readjust   [1 mark]
7. interrelated   [1 mark]
8. rebuild   [1 mark]

Try these

The children write definitions for words. Tell them to use their knowledge of the root word and the prefix to

predict the meaning before checking in the dictionary if necessary.

Possible answers
Accept all correct definitions, for example:
1. *to write something again*   *[example]*
2. respond to something   [1 mark]
3. to adjust or move again   [1 mark]
4. to dial again   [1 mark]
5. between countries   [1 mark]
6. to move things around or tidy   [1 mark]
7. to act or work together   [1 mark]
8. exchangeable   [1 mark]

Now try these

The children compose sentences using the target words 'reread', 'rewrap', 'rewind', 'relive', 'intermingle', 'intermission', 'intersection', 'interview'. Read the words together and ensure that the children understand the meaning of each. Share the children's sentences.

Answers

Jacob has <u>reread</u> *his favourite book five times.*   *[example]*

Accept any sentences where the target word is correctly spelt and used. [8 marks: 1 mark per sentence]

Support, embed & challenge

Support

Ask these children to complete Unit 6 Resource 1: <u>Inter</u>connected meanings. Discuss the meanings of the words and work together to compose a sentence for each word. (**Answers** react – respond to something; interrupt – speak when someone else is talking; intervene – take action to improve a bad situation; rewrite – change what was written before; remove – take away or get rid of; international – of or involving more than one nation; rename – give something a new name; reappear – become visible again; intercity – route from one city to another; review – give an opinion on how good a thing is; redeliver – attempt to deliver again; interfere – meddle with something; reassemble – put back together; rebuild – construct or build again; internet – network linking computers worldwide)

Give pairs of children the word cards (see Additional resources) along with multiple 're–' and 'inter–' cards, and ask them to create some words using the prefixes and root words. Share the words the pairs have found and discuss the meaning of each. Discuss the difference between 'interview' and 'review' if they come up.

Embed

Ask the children to complete Unit 6 Resource 2: Prefix mix. When they have completed the task, share the words they have found, creating a long list. (**Answers** replace, displace, misplace, reshape, misshape, rematch, mismatch, recover, discover, inaction, reaction, reconnect, disconnect, misconnect, reassemble, disassemble, misassemble, refit, misfit, relocate, dislocate, rename, misname, reorganised, disorganised, intake, retake, mistake, reappear, disappear, inactive, reactive, replant, inability, disability)

Challenge

These children may have noticed that there are not many examples of words beginning with the prefix 'inter–'. Explain that these words are not as common as the words beginning 're–'. Ask these children to find as many words beginning 'inter–' as they can, such as 'intercom', 'interpretation', 'interval', 'interpreter', 'intersection', 'interplay', 'interlocking' and 'intersect'. Ask them to share the words they have found with the class.

Homework / Additional activities

Spelling test

Ask the children to learn one of the following lists of words for a spelling test. Challenge them to write sentences for five of the words on their list.

Core words		Support words		Challenge words	
react	redeliver	react	rebuild	react	reconsider
rebuild	intercity	replace	intercity	rebuild	reroute
remove	interfere	remove	interfere	remove	intercity
rename	internet	rename	internet	rename	interfere
rewrite	interrupt	rewrite	international	rewrite	internet
reappear	international			reappear	interrupt
review	intervene			review	international
reassemble				reassemble	intervene
				redeliver	interrelated
				recall	interact

Collins Connect: Unit 6

Ask the children to complete Unit 6 (see Teach → Year 4 → Spelling → Unit 6).

Unit 7: The prefixes sub– and super–

Overview

English curriculum objectives
- More prefixes

Treasure House resources
- Spelling Skills Pupil Book 4, Unit 7, pages 16–17
- Collins Connect Treasure House Spelling Year 4, Unit 7
- Photocopiable Unit 7, Resource 1: Super spellings, page 96

- Photocopiable Unit 7, Resource 2: Don't subscribe to substandard spelling!, page 97

Additional resources
- Word cards: submarine, subheading, subtitle, submerge, subservient, substandard, subgroup, subset, subcontinent, subscribe, supercar, superhero, supermarket, superglue, superstar

Introduction

Teaching overview
The prefix 'sub–' means 'under' or 'less', for example, 'subheading', 'subordinate'; the prefix 'super–' means 'over', 'beyond' or 'greater', for example, 'superhero', 'superpowers'.

Introduce the concept
Write the word 'supermarket' on the board. Ask: 'What is so super about a 'supermarket'?' Discuss the difference between a 'market' and a 'supermarket'. Ask the children if they can think of any other 'super–' words. Encourage them to remember the work they did on this prefix in Year 3.

Collect as many 'super–' words from the children as you can, for example, 'supercar', 'superpowers', 'superman' and 'supervision'. Have fun discussing the super abilities of various superheroes.

Ask: 'Who can remember what the prefix 'sub–' means?' Agree that this means 'below' or 'less important'. Ask the children to think of 'sub–' words, encouraging them to remember the work they did on this prefix in Year 3. Collect as many 'sub–' words from the children as you can and write them on the board, for example, 'submarine', 'subheading', 'subtitle', 'submerge', 'subservient', 'substandard' and 'subgroup'.

Pupil practice

Pupil Book pages 16–17

Get started
The children separate words into their prefixes and roots. Read the words with children and check for understanding. Afterwards, use the prefixes to talk further about the meanings of the words.

Answers
1. super / market	[example]
2. sub / divide	[1 mark]
3. sub / section	[1 mark]
4. super / heated	[1 mark]
5. sub / ordinate	[1 mark]
6. sub / class	[1 mark]
7. super / bug	[1 mark]
8. super / charge	[1 mark]

Try these
The children add the prefixes 'sub–' or 'super–' to root words. Tell the children to try out both prefixes with the root word, saying each new word out loud

before deciding which word is the one that exists in English.

Answers
1. *supermarket*	*[example]*
2. superimpose	[1 mark]
3. submarine	[1 mark]
4. submerge	[1 mark]
5. substandard	[1 mark]
6. subcontinent	[1 mark]
7. subtropical	[1 mark]
8. superheated	[1 mark]

Now try these
The children compose sentences to use the target words 'subsection', 'supermarket', 'superstar', 'subheading', 'submarine', 'subcontract', 'submerge' and 'superglue'. Read the words together and ensure that the children understand the meanings. Share the children's sentences.

Answers

The Sunday newspaper had many different *subsections.* *[example]*

Accept any sentences where the target word is correctly spelt and used. [8 marks: 1 mark per sentence]

Support, embed & challenge

Support

Ask the children to complete Unit 7 Resource 1: Super spellings. (**Answers** submarine, superhero, subheading, superstar, subway, subscribe, superheated, submerge, superset (mathematical term), subset, subdivide, superstore, superpower, subtract)

Discuss the children's answers and talk about the meanings of the words, using the meanings of the prefixes and root words to predict the meanings of any words they are not sure about.

As a group, make up new words that begin with 'super–' for use in a superhero story, for example, 'superskates', 'superjump' and 'superspecs'. Add 'sub–' to words to create silly attributes or equipment for a useless sidekick called 'Subkid', such as 'subvision' and 'subcharge'.

Read the word cards together (see Additional resources), sorting them into 'super–' and 'sub–' words. Present the cards spread out upside down and ask each child to choose a card. Give them a few moments to read their card and then to make up a sentence using the word.

Embed

Ask the children to complete Unit 7 Resource 2: Don't subscribe to substandard spelling! (**Answers** 1. submerged, 2. superglue, 3. subdivided, 4. supercar, 5. superstar, 6. subsection, 7. submarine, 8. supermarket)

Organise the children into teams and challenge the teams to write as many 'sub–' and 'super–' words as they can in two minutes. Award a point for each correct word and a second point for each word that no other team has. Award a bonus point for the longest word.

Ask the groups to investigate the meanings of the words 'subconscious', 'subordinate' and 'subcontinent' and then share their findings.

Challenge

Challenge these children to create a comic strip science fiction story using the words 'antimatter', 'subspace', 'supernova', 'intergalactic' and 'interstellar'.

Homework / Additional activities

Spelling test

Ask the children to learn one of the following lists of words for a spelling test. Challenge them to write sentences for five of the words on their list.

Core words		Support words		Challenge words	
supermarket	subheading	supermarket	subheading	supermarket	submerge
superhero	subtitle	superhero	subtitle	superhero	subtitle
superpower	submarine	superpower	submarine	superpower	subway
superstar	submerge	supersonic	subway	superstar	subdued
supersonic	subway	supercar	subtract	supersonic	subdivide
supercar	subsection			superintendent	subsequent
supervise	subtract			supercar	subscribe
superglue	subdivide			supervision	subtitle
				superglue	subsection
				subheading	subtract
				submarine	

Collins Connect: Unit 7

Ask the children to complete Unit 7 (see Teach → Year 4 → Spelling → Unit 7).

Unit 8: The prefixes anti– and auto–

Overview

English curriculum objectives
* More prefixes

Treasure House resources
* Spelling Skills Pupil Book 4, Unit 8, pages 18–19
* Collins Connect Treasure House Spelling Year 4, Unit 8
* Photocopiable Unit 8, Resource 1: <u>Automatically spell correctly</u>, page 98

* Photocopiable Unit 8, Resource 2: <u>Auto–</u> or <u>anti–</u>?, page 99

Additional resources
* Word cards: antibacterial, antibiotics, anticlimax, anticlockwise, antidote, antifreeze, antihero, antiseptic, antisocial, antiserum, autobiography, autograph, automatic, automobile, autopilot
* Blank cards for the children to create flash cards

Introduction

Teaching overview

The prefix 'anti–' means 'against'. The words that start with this prefix are, in the main, rather difficult for Year 4 children. But, having encountered them already in Year 3, they will, hopefully, understand the words and how they are constructed even if they are not regularly using them.

The prefix 'auto–' means 'oneself'. There are only five words that are suitable for Year 4 children: 'autobiography', 'autograph', 'automatic', 'autopilot' and perhaps 'automobile'.

Introduce the concept

Write the words 'autograph' and 'anticlimax' on the board. Ask the children to look at the words and

think about how they are constructed. Ask volunteers to split each word into prefix and root. Remind the children that, though many of these words are quite obscure, they have studied them before in Year 3. Organise the children into groups. Ask the groups to try to recall as many words as they can with these two prefixes. Give out the word cards (see Additional resources) to random children in the class and ask them to keep their word secret and stand up. Ask each group to read out the words that they have listed. Write them on the board, separating the 'auto–' words from the 'anti–' words. Ask the children with cards to sit down when their word is said. At the end, ask the children still standing to write their words in the correct list. Discuss the meaning of each word.

Pupil practice

Pupil Book pages 18–19

Get started

The children split words into their prefixes and roots. Read the words together and discuss the meanings of 'automobile' (car), 'antioxidant' (something that keeps us healthy), 'antiglare' (something that stops thing glaring in your eyes), 'antithesis' (complete opposite), 'autodidact' (person who has taught themselves), 'autotimer' (something that is programmed to come on and go off).

Answers

1. *auto / mobile*   *[example]*
2. anti / oxidant   [1 mark]
3. anti / glare   [1 mark]
4. anti / thesis   [1 mark]
5. auto / graph   [1 mark]
6. auto / pilot   [1 mark]
7. auto / didact   [1 mark]
8. auto / timer   [1 mark]

Try these

The children add the prefixes 'anti–' or 'auto–' to root words. Tell the children to try out both prefixes with the root word, saying each new word out loud before deciding which word is the one that exists in English. Afterwards, discuss the meaning of each word, in particular 'antiseptic', 'antidote', 'antibacterial', 'antiviral', 'antibody' and 'antimatter'. (You might just want to say that 'antimatter' is a complicated concept in physics!)

Answers

1. <u>anti</u>septic   *[example]*
2. <u>auto</u>mobile   [1 mark]
3. <u>auto</u>biography   [1 mark]
4. <u>anti</u>dote   [1 mark]
5. <u>anti</u>matter   [1 mark]
6. <u>anti</u>bacterial   [1 mark]
7. <u>anti</u>viral   [1 mark]
8. <u>anti</u>body   [1 mark]

Now try these

The children compose sentences using the target words 'antiseptic', 'antidote', 'autopilot', 'automaton', 'anticlimax', 'autograph', 'antihero' and 'antisocial'. Read the words together and ensure that the children understand their meanings. Share the children's sentences.

Answers

Emma cleaned her graze with antiseptic lotion.   [example]

Accept any sentences where the target word is correctly spelt and used. [8 marks: 1 mark per sentence]

Support, embed & challenge

Support

Use the most straightforward word cards with these children: 'autograph', 'autopilot', 'autobiography', 'automatic', 'antifreeze', 'anticlockwise'. Read each word and then cut up each word card into root word and prefix. Muddle up the cards and recreate the words. Discuss the meaning of each word.

Ask the children to complete Unit 8 Resource 1: Automatically spell correctly. (**Answers** automatic – moves or activates on its own; anticlockwise – opposite to the direction clock hands travel; autobiography – story of your own life; antisocial – behaviour that is bad for others; antifreeze – liquid that stops things freezing; antidote – medicine that treats poison; autopilot – do something without thinking; antiseptic – stops or prevents infection; automobile – an old-fashioned word for a car; autograph – signature of someone important;)

Embed

Ask the children to complete Unit 8 Resource 2: Auto– or anti–? (**Answers** 1. anticlimax, 2. anticlockwise, 3. antifreeze, 4. autobiography, 5. autograph, 6. autopilot, 7. antisocial, 8. antiseptic)

Reassure the children that, yes, many of these words are difficult but that, if they use their knowledge of prefixes, they should be able to understand most of their meanings. Encourage them to enjoy learning these words, challenging them to use them in other lessons and contexts during the week.

Provide the children with blank cards and challenge them to investigate the meanings of the words 'autodidact' (someone who is self taught), 'antithesis' (the complete opposite), 'antiviral' (a drug that attacks viruses), 'automaton' (an early robot), 'antimatter' (opposite of matter) and, the longest word in the English language, 'antidisestablishmentarianism' (being against the people who are against the Queen being the head of the Church of England). Tell the children to create flash cards for the words, writing the word on one side and the meaning on the other. Explain that they can probably get through their lives happily without using these words but that they might enjoy bamboozling their parents with their sophisticated vocabulary.

Challenge

Explain to these children that the prefix 'anti–' can be used to create new words. Ask them to discuss what it might mean to be 'anti-car' or 'anti-technology'. Ask them to make up their own sentences using new 'anti–' words of their own creation such as: 'My mum is anti-sweets, anti-computers and anti-noise; in fact she's plain anti-fun.'

Homework / Additional activities

Spelling test

Ask the children to learn one of the following lists of words for a spelling test. Challenge them to write sentences for five of the words on their list.

Core words		Support words		Challenge words	
anticlockwise	autobiography	anticlockwise	autobiography	anticlockwise	antibiotics
antifreeze	autograph	antifreeze	autograph	antifreeze	antihero
antidote	automatic	antidote	automatic	antidote	autobiography
antiseptic	automobile	antiseptic	automobile	antiseptic	autograph
antisocial	autopilot	antisocial	autopilot	antisocial	automatic
anticlimax				anticlimax	autopilot
				antibacterial	

Collins Connect: Unit 8

Ask the children to complete Unit 8 (see Teach → Year 4 → Spelling → Unit 8).

Review unit 1

A. Ask the children to correctly spell each word.

1. myth [1 mark]

2. occurred [1 mark]

3. courageous [1 mark]

4. illegal [1 mark]

5. syrup [1 mark]

6. enough [1 mark]

7. misspell [1 mark]

8. impossible [1 mark]

9. bicycle [1 mark]

10. couple [1 mark]

B. Ask the children to choose the correct spelling of each word.

1. forgotten [1 mark]

2. courage [1 mark]

3. glorious [1 mark]

4. interview [1 mark]

5. mistaken [1 mark]

6. transferring [1 mark]

7. automatic [1 mark]

8. listened [1 mark]

C. Ask the children to use the prefixes 'dis–', 'mis–', 'ir–', 'im–', 'super–', 'sub–' or 'auto–' with the bold word in each phrase to write a word that matches the meaning of the phrase.

1. impatient [1 mark]

2. dishonest [1 mark]

3. misjudge [1 mark]

4. irrelevant [1 mark]

5. supermarket [1 mark]

6. antiseptic [1 mark]

7. subcontinent [1 mark]

8. substandard [1 mark]

 # Unit 9: The suffix –ation

Overview

English curriculum objectives
- The suffix –ation

Treasure House resources
- Spelling Skills Pupil Book 4, Unit 9, pages 22–23
- Collins Connect Treasure House Spelling Year 4, Unit 9
- Photocopiable Unit 9, Resource 1: An –ation examination, page 100

- Photocopiable Unit 9, Resource 2: Experimentation in adding –ation, page 101

Additional resources
- Word cards: e, information, adoration, sensation, preparation, admiration, limitation, inspiration, exploration, observation, compilation, reservation, conservation, determination, organisation, examination, continuation, temptation, adaptation
- Dice

Introduction

Teaching overview

The suffix '–ation' can be used to turn verbs into nouns, for example, 'prepare' → 'preparation'. The suffix can be added directly to many verbs, such as 'inform' → 'information'. However, for verbs ending 'e', the 'e' needs to be removed, for example, 'admire' → 'admiration'. There are many words ending in '–ation' where the root word is changed in other ways, but this unit focusses on words where the verb–noun relationship is straightforward.

Introduce the concept

Ask children to work in pairs and give each pair one of the word cards (see Additional resources). Ask them to read the word together and discuss its meaning. Ask: 'What sort of word have you been given: a noun, a verb or an adjective?' Agree that the words are nouns and remind the children that they can check this by putting 'the' in front of their

word and checking it makes sense. Challenge them to turn their noun into a verb. Suggest that they try putting 'we' in front of their word and decide how it needs to change in order to sound right. Write the word 'confrontation' on the board and model the process of changing 'confrontation' to 'confront'. Explain that you have just removed the suffix '–ation'. Repeat the process with 'continuation', resulting in 'continu'. Explain that you need to add an 'e' to complete this word. Ask the children to look at their word cards again then turn them over and write the corresponding verb on the back. Tell the children to place their card verb-side up and then stand up. Ask them to move around the room in their pairs and look at each verb displayed. Tell them to discuss with their partner what the corresponding noun would be and how it would be spelt before turning over the card to check. Tell them to leave the new card verb-side up for the next pair and move on to another card.

Pupil practice

Pupil Book pages 22–23

Get started

The children identify and write the root verb for nouns ending '–ation'. Read the words with the children and ensure that they know the meaning of each. Recap on the noun–verb relationship in this situation and the possible need to add an 'e' to the end of the root word. Afterwards, demonstrate the change in meaning, for example: 'Mum altered my dress. I was pleased with the alteration.' Afterwards, discuss which words needed an 'e' adding and how they knew to add it.

Answers

1. *alter*		*[example]*
2. confront		[1 mark]
3. tempt		[1 mark]
4. condense		[1 mark]
5. accuse		[1 mark]
6. sense		[1 mark]
7. preserve		[1 mark]
8. repute		[1 mark]

Try these

The children choose the correct spellings for words ending with the suffix '–ation'. Remind the children that words with 'e' at the end need this 'e' removed before the '–ation' suffix is added. Ask them to look at the two options and choose the correct option, remembering this rule.

Answers

1. *determination*   *[example]*
2. compilation   [1 mark]
3. reformation   [1 mark]
4. conservation   [1 mark]
5. determination   [1 mark]
6. infestation   [1 mark]
7. obligation   [1 mark]
8. colonisation   [1 mark]

Now try these

The children compose sentences to use the target words 'condensation', 'alteration', 'frustration', 'temptation', 'information' and 'inclination'. Read the words together and ensure that the children understand the meaning of each. Afterwards, share the children's sentences.

Answers

The windows were wet from <u>condensation</u>. *[example]*

Accept any sentences where the target word is correctly spelt and used in the correct context. [6 marks: 1 mark per sentence]

Support, embed & challenge

Support

Work with these children with a set of word cards (see Additional resources). Read the words together and discuss whether the words are easy or difficult to spell. Take the words 'information', 'limitation', 'temptation' and 'adaptation' and cut off the '–ation' ending. Read the root words together and ask: 'Are these words easier to spell?' Practise spelling the '–ation' ending together, then practise spelling the root words. Finally, practise putting the root words and suffix together and spelling the whole words. Move on to the remaining words. Cut off the ends of the words and discuss what the original root word would have been. Introduce the 'e' card and model swapping between the 'e' and '–ation' endings.

Ask the children to complete Unit 9 Resource 1: An –<u>ation</u> examin<u>ation</u>. (**Answers 1.** *information [example]*, **2.** temptation, **3.** inspiration, **4.** preparation, **5.** examination, **6.** observation, **7.** organisation, **8.** exploration; **1.** reserve, **2.** expect, **3.** recommend, **4.** declare)

Embed

Organise the children into groups of no more than six children. Give each group a dice and a set of word cards: either the word cards or words from Unit 9 Resource 2: Experiment<u>ation</u> in adding –<u>ation</u>, if they are very confident in spelling the words on the words cards. Tell them to allocate a number to each child in the group and then put the cards face down in a pile. Tell them to take turns to roll the dice. The child whose number is rolled must take a card, read the word pass it to their neighbour and attempt to spell it. If they spell it correctly, they keep the card.

Ask the children to complete Unit 9 Resource 2: Experiment<u>ation</u> in adding –<u>ation</u>. (**Answers** invitation, transform, installation, inspire, destination, confirm, documentation, starve, experimentation, deprive, adaptation, realise, civilisation, transport, inclination, modernise, notation, organisation)

Challenge

Ask these children to research the meanings of any unfamiliar '–ation' words in the Pupil Book (pages 22–23). Challenge them to find four new words ending '–ation' not covered in these activities.

Homework / Additional activities

Spelling test

Ask the children to learn one of the following lists of words for a spelling test. Challenge them to write sentences for five of the words on their list.

Core words		Support words		Challenge words	
information	conversation	information	examination	information	determination
invitation	observation	invitation	organisation	invitation	inspiration
destination	determination	destination	conversation	destination	confirmation
preparation	inspiration	preparation	observation	preparation	realisation
exploration	confirmation	exploration	inspiration	exploration	adaptation
examination	realisation			examination	conservation
organisation	adaptation			organisation	starvation
				conversation	modernisation
				observation	transformation

Collins Connect: Unit 9

Ask the children to complete Unit 9 (see Teach → Year 4 → Spelling → Unit 9).

 # Unit 10: The suffix –ly

Overview

English curriculum objectives
- The suffix –ly

Treasure House resources
- Spelling Skills Pupil Book 4, Unit 10, pages 24–25
- Collins Connect Treasure House Spelling Year 4, Unit 10
- Photocopiable Unit 10, Resource 1: Adverb pairs, page 102

- Photocopiable Unit 10, Resource 2: Skilfully and capably spelling words ending –ly, page 103

Additional resources
- Word cards: wide, safe, slow, hopeless, tireless, endless, guilty, moody, gloomy, gentle, possible, horrible, favourable, humble, simple, automatic, specific

Introduction

Teaching overview

By now, the children should be quite secure in adding '–ly' to words that end in 'y' ('cheery' → 'cheerily'). Across Years 3 and 4, the focus is on adding '–ly' to a wider range of words, for example, those that end 'le' and 'ic'. There are four rules for adding '–ly'.

1. Most words: Just add '–ly', for example, 'careful' → 'carefully', 'polite' → 'politely'. (The final 'l' in 'careful' and final 'e' in 'polite' are retained.)

2. Words ending in 'y': remove the 'y' and add 'i', for example, 'grumpy' → 'grumpily'.

3. Words ending in 'le': remove the 'le', for example, 'wrinkle' → 'wrinkly'.

4. Words ending in 'ic': add 'ally', for example, 'automatic' → 'automatically'.

Of course, some words break the rules. These words, such as 'truly' and 'wholly', just have to be learned.

Most (but not all) of these words are adverbs.

Introduce the concept

Ask for some brave volunteers. Give each volunteer one of the following words on a slip of paper: 'dramatically', 'horribly', 'happily', 'quickly', 'politely', 'carefully'. Tell them to go out of the class and then come back in, moving or behaving in the way their word describes. After each performance, help the rest of the class to guess the adverb. Ask the child whose word it was to write it on the board.

Together, decide what the corresponding adjective would be for each adverb ('dramatic', 'horrible', 'happy', 'quick', 'polite' and 'careful'). Write each adjective next to its adverb. For each pair of words, ask: 'How did this adjective change when '–ly' was added?' Use the words to illustrate the four spelling rules. Ask: 'Why does 'carefully' end '–lly'?' Agree that '–ly' has been added to a word ending in 'l'. Point out that 'politely' has not lost its 'e'.

Pupil practice

Pupil Book pages 24–25

Get started

The children add '–ally' or '–ly' to words, writing them in the correct column of a table. Before they do so, read the introduction to the spelling pattern in the Pupil Book, ensuring that the children understand what happens to words ending 'ic' when '–ly' is added. After the children have completed the chart, ask how they added '–ly' to words ending 'le'.

Answers

Words ending in '–ally'		Words ending in '–ly'	
comically	[example]	humbly	[1 mark]
historically	[1 mark]	ably	[1 mark]
critically	[1 mark]	scribbly	[1 mark]
logically	[1 mark]	terribly	[1 mark]

Try these

The children change the adjective into an adverb by adding the correct suffix. Ask the children to remember all the rules they have learned and add the suffix to each of the given words. Afterwards, ask the children what they had to do in each case.

Answers

1. *energetically*	*[example]*
2. heroically	[1 mark]
3. usually	[1 mark]
4. happily	[1 mark]
5. poetically	[1 mark]
6. nobly	[1 mark]
7. greedily	[1 mark]

Now try these

The children compose sentences using the target words 'brightly', 'skilfully', 'sumptuously', 'happily', 'frantically', 'truly', 'wholly' and 'realistically'. Read the words together and ensure that the children understand the meaning of each. Afterwards, share the children's sentences.

Answers

The sun shone <u>brightly</u>. [example]

Accept any sentences where the target word is correctly spelt and used. [8 marks: 1 mark per sentence]

Support, embed & challenge

Support

Ask these children to complete Unit 10 Resource 1: Adverb pairs. Afterwards, discuss the changes made to each adjective to turn it into an adverb. Help the children to see the words where 'e' has been removed (those ending 'le') and those where the 'e' has been retained (all other words). Locate words that retained their final 'l' thus creating an '–lly' ending. (**Answers** just add '–ly': childish – childishly, painful – painfully, entire – entirely, close – closely; remove 'le' then add '–ly': horrible – horribly, sensible – sensibly, terrible – terribly; turn 'y' into 'i' then add '–ly': steady – steadily, healthy – healthily, grumpy – grumpily; add '–ally': basic – basically, terrific – terrifically, frantic – frantically)

Look at the word cards together (see Additional resources). Ask the children to help you spell the adverb for each adjective. Write the adverbs on the backs of the cards. Display the cards adjective-side up and challenge each child, in turn, to choose a card and tell the rest of the group how to add '–ly'. They should then turn over the card to see if they are correct.

Embed

Write the words 'automatic', 'logic', 'specific', 'dramatic', 'terrific', 'frantic' and 'critic' on the board. Ask the children to write the corresponding adverbs on their whiteboards. Ask one of the children to read out the adverbs they have written. Discuss the pronunciation of each and whether the /a/ is clearly heard. Explain that often the /a/ sound is lost and this can make us forget it when spelling. Point out that we might say /logicly/ but we must remember to write 'logically'.

Ask the children to complete Unit 10 Resource 2: Skilful<u>ly</u> and capab<u>ly</u> spelling words ending –l<u>y</u>. (**Answers** 1. basically, 2. entirely, 3. terrifically, 4. wobbly, 5. prickly, 6. acrobatically, 7. enthusiastically, 8. politely, 9. painfully, 10. quickly)

Challenge

Ask these children to create a list of interesting adverbs that they want to use in their writing.

Challenge them to investigate words ending '–ically' and write down their favourites.

Homework / Additional activities

Spelling test

Ask the children to learn one of the following lists of words for a spelling test. Challenge them to write sentences for five of the words on their list.

Core words		Support words		Challenge words	
easily	horribly	easily	simply	angrily	basically
busily	simply	busily	basically	busily	comically
noisily	basically	noisily	comically	noisily	terrifically
steadily	comically	closely	carefully	entirely	logically
entirely	terrifically	wobbly	painfully	closely	heroically
closely	carefully			wobbly	energetically
wobbly	painfully			horribly	dramatically
				simply	carefully
				crumbly	painfully

Collins Connect: Unit 10

Ask the children to complete Unit 10 (see Teach → Year 4 → Spelling → Unit 10).

Unit 11: The ending –sure

Overview

English curriculum objectives
- Words with endings sounding like /zhur/ or /cher/

Treasure House resources
- Spelling Skills Pupil Book 4, Unit 11, pages 26–27
- Collins Connect Treasure House Spelling Year 4, Unit 11
- Photocopiable Unit 11, Resource 1: Letter match, page 104

- Photocopiable Unit 11, Resource 2: It's a pleasure spelling sure, page 105

Additional resources
- Word cards: closure, composure, disclosure, displeasure, enclosure, exposure, leisure, measure, pleasure, treasure
- Bags to draw letter cards from (for Resource 1)

Introduction

Teaching overview

There are a few words in English that end in a buzzy /zhur/ sound, for example, 'treasure' and 'measure'. This ending is always spelt '–sure' and needs to be distinguished from the /sher/ ending, which is usually spelt '–sher' as in 'blusher'. It is important that the children can hear the distinction before attempting this spelling. There are a few words that slightly confuse this rule, such as 'assure', 'reassure' and 'pressure' that have the /sher/ ending spelt '–ssure', 'insure' that has the /shor/ ending spelt '–sure' and 'censure' that has the /sher/ ending spelt '–sure'.

Introduce the concept

Say the words 'measure', 'treasure' and 'leisure' and ask the children what these words have in common. Agree they all have the /zhur/ ending spelt '–sure'.

Ask the children if they can think of any other words with this ending. Encourage them to remember the work they did on this spelling pattern in Year 3. Write their suggestions on the board and point out the '–sure' spelling. Explain that, if they hear a /zhur/ ending, it is spelt '–sure'. Compare this ending to the /sher/ ending of 'dishwasher'. Explain that the /sher/ ending is usually spelt '–sher'.

Tell the children to write '–sure' on one side of their whiteboards and '–sher' on the other. Say a range of words with both the /sher/ and /zhur/ endings, for example, 'measure', dishwasher', 'leisure', 'fisher', 'closure', 'fresher', 'exposure', 'flusher', 'treasure', 'finisher', 'enclosure', 'posher', 'pleasure' and 'wisher'. Ask the children hold up the correct spelling for the ending of each word. Write each word on the board, grouping the two endings.

Pupil practice

Pupil Book pages 26–27

Get started

The children discern whether words are spelt correctly or not. They copy the correctly spelt words into the first column of a table and write the misspelt words in the second column, correcting the mistakes. Remind the children that the /zhur/ sound is always spelt '–sure'.

Answers

Correctly spelt words		Corrected words	
pleasure	[example]	measure	[1 mark]
treasure	[1 mark]	enclosure	[1 mark]
closure	[1 mark]	composure	[1 mark]
leisure	[1 mark]	discomposure	[1 mark]

Try these

The children rearrange jumbled letters to spell words ending '–sure'. Tell the children to remember the '–sure' spelling pattern. Advise them to start with the '–sure' ending of each word and then see what letters they have left.

Answers

1. composure		[example]
2. displeasure		[1 mark]
3. treasure		[1 mark]
4. disclosure		[1 mark]
5. leisure		[1 mark]
6. exposure		[1 mark]

Now try these

The children compose sentences using the target words 'enclosure', 'displeasure', 'pleasure', 'composure', 'closure', 'exposure' and 'treasure'. Read the words together and ensure that the children understand the meaning of each. Tell the children to share their ideas with a partner before writing. Afterwards, share the children's sentences.

Answers

The children looked at the chickens in their wire *enclosure. [example]*

Accept any sentences where the target word is correctly spelt and used. [7 marks: 1 mark per sentence]

Support, embed & challenge

Support

Play the game on Unit 11 Resource 1: Letter match, with the children.

Have a list of words ending /sher/ and /zhur/, for example, 'measure', dishwasher', 'leisure', 'fisher', 'closure', 'fresher', 'exposure', 'flusher', 'treasure', 'finisher', 'enclosure', 'posher', 'pleasure' and 'wisher'. Read out the words one at a time, emphasising the difference in the endings. Ask the children to work together to spell each word. Remind them that the ending should be straightforward: either '–sher' or '–sure'. Have the children write the words as two lists.

Embed

Explain to the children that, although the /zhur/ sound is always spelt '–sure', the '–sure' ending is not always pronounced /zhur/. In a few words the /sher/ ending can also be spelt '–sure' or '–ssure'. Write 'pressure', 'reassure', 'assure', 'insure', 'ensure' and 'sure' and read these words together. Ask the children to spend a few minutes memorising these

words. Ask them to write '–sure' on one side of their whiteboards and '–ssure' on the other. Read out the words 'measure', 'crusher', 'leisure', 'pressure', 'well-wisher', 'closure', 'fresher', 'ensure', 'exposure', 'treasure', 'reassure', 'enclosure', 'posher', 'pleasure' and 'sure'. For each word, ask the children to hold up the appropriate ending or, if the ending is '–sher', nothing at all.

Ask the children to complete Unit 11 Resource 2: It's a plea**sure** spelling <u>sure</u>. (**Answers** 1. leisure, 2. pleasure, 3. pressure, 4. fresher, 5. treasure, 6. enclosure, 7. crusher, 8. closure)

Challenge

Challenge these children to research the meanings of 'ensure' and 'insure'.

Ask these children to write a story (or story opener) using the words 'treasure', 'measure', 'closure', 'exposure' and 'pressure'.

Homework / Additional activities

Spelling test

Ask the children to learn one of the following lists of words for a spelling test. Challenge them to write sentences for five of the words on their list.

Core words		Support words		Challenge words	
closure	exposure	closure	exposure	closure	measure
composure	leisure	composure	leisure	composure	pleasure
disclosure	measure	disclosure	measure	disclosure	treasure
displeasure	pleasure	displeasure	pleasure	displeasure	assure
enclosure	treasure	enclosure	treasure	enclosure	reassure
				exposure	pressure
				leisure	insure

Collins Connect: Unit 11

Ask the children to complete Unit 11 (see Teach → Year 4 → Spelling → Unit 11).

Unit 12: The endings –ture, –cher and –tcher

Overview

English curriculum objectives
- Words with endings sounding like /zhur/ or /cher/

Treasure House resources
- Spelling Skills Pupil Book 4, Unit 12, pages 28–29
- Collins Connect Treasure House Spelling Year 4, Unit 12
- Photocopiable Unit 12, Resource 1: Nurture your knowledge of –ture, page 106
- Photocopiable Unit 12, Resource 2: A crossword adventure, page 107

Additional resources
- Word cards: mixture, departure, capture, adventure, nature, picture, future, creature, feature, temperature, furniture, miniature, puncture, moisture, vulture, immature, signature, texture, sculpture, sketcher, thatcher, catcher, snatcher, pitcher, watcher, stretcher, teacher, preacher, marcher, richer, searcher
- Gridded paper

Introduction

Teaching overview
The /cher/ sound at the end of a word can be spelt '–cher', '–tcher' or '–ture'. The three endings are equally common in English, though the words with '–ture' are possibly more useful. The children should be aware that they are making a choice between these three endings when writing.

Introduce the concept
Write the endings '–ture', '–tcher' and '–cher' on the board. Give each child one of the word cards (see Additional resources) and ask them which of these endings their word has. Ask them to stand up and sort themselves into three sets: one for each ending.

Write the words from the cards on the board in three columns. Read the words together and agree that they all have the same sound at the end. Explain that we need to learn when to use which spelling. Ask them to sit back down, turn to a partner and tell that partner what their word means. Once they have done so, ask if anyone can describe their word by starting with or including the words 'someone who ...', for example: 'A "teacher" is someone who teaches.' Find these words on the board, and emphasise the point by drawing a line between the root verbs and the '–er' endings, for example 'teach/er'. Explain that, when spelling a word that is not a root verb plus '–er', then the spelling is most likely to be '–ture' at the end.

Pupil practice

Pupil Book pages 28–29

Get started
The children sort words into two groups according to how the /cher/ sound is spelt: '–ture' or '–cher'/ '–tcher'. Ask the children to read each word, ensuring that they can hear the /cher/ sound. Discuss the meaning of any unknown words such as 'gesture', 'pasture' and 'agriculture'.

Answers

'–ture'		'–cher' / '–tcher'	
adventure	[example]	richer	[1 mark]
pasture	[1 mark]	catcher	[1 mark]
agriculture	[1 mark]		
signature	[1 mark]		
gesture	[1 mark]		
departure	[1 mark]		

Try these
The children choose the correct spellings of words. Afterwards, agree on the correct spelling of each word and ask the children how they knew which ending to choose. Discuss the near-homophones 'picture' and 'pitcher'.

Answers
1. *texture* [example]
2. architecture [1 mark]
3. watcher [1 mark]
4. lecture [1 mark]
5. pitcher [1 mark]
6. feature [1 mark]
7. stretcher [1 mark]
8. nurture [1 mark]

Now try these

The children compose sentences using the target words 'agriculture', 'departure', 'fracture', 'vulture', 'gesture', 'future', 'sculpture' and 'puncture'. Read the words together and ensure that the children understand the meaning of each. Tell the children to share their ideas with a partner before writing. Afterwards, share the children's sentences.

Answers

Agriculture is the science or practice of farming.   *[example]*

Accept any sentences where the target word is correctly spelt and used. [8 marks: 1 mark per sentence]

Support, embed & challenge

Support

Look at the word cards together (see Additional resources). Ask the children to sort them into two piles: words ending '–ture' and words ending '–tcher' or '–cher'. Put the '–ture' words to one side and look at the other words. Display all the '–tcher' and '–cher' words and choose one. Cut the '–er' ending off the word and read it. Agree that it is now a verb and still a whole word. Put the '–er' back on. Ask each child in turn to choose a word, read it then cut off the '–er' and say what the remaining word is. Return to the '–ture' words. Cut the '–ure' ending off one of the '–ture' words to demonstrate that you will not be left with anything useful.

Put the cards with words ending '–ture' in the middle of the group and read them together. Ask the children to close their eyes and tell you the last four letters of each word. Deal out the cards and ask each child in turn to read their card. Tell them to pass their cards to the person on their left. Ask everyone to read their cards aloud. Pass the cards on and read them a couple more times. Take in the cards. Ask each child in turn to say one of the words and to try spelling it. Carry on until all the words on the word cards have been spelt.

Ask the children to complete Unit 12 Resource 1: Nur<u>ture</u> your knowledge of –ture. (**Answers** 1. mixture, 2. departure, 3. recapture, 4. creature, 5. nature, 6. picture, 7. adventure, 8. future)

Embed

Ask the children to work in pairs and give each pair a set of word cards (see Additional resources). Tell them to take turns to read the words to each other. Without looking, the listener must say whether the word ends '–ture', '–tcher' or '–cher'. The reader puts the words into three piles. Afterwards, the listener checks the piles to see how well they have done.

Provide the children with gridded paper. Tell them to use the words in their spelling test list (see Spelling test) to create a word search. They should then swap word searches with someone and both complete each other's word searches.

Ask the children to complete Unit 12 Resource 2: A crossword adven<u>ture</u>. (**Answers** Across: 2. temperature, 4. vulture, 5. miniature, 6. puncture, 9. picture, 10. gesture; Down: 1. immature, 3. adventure, 7. capture, 8. signature)

Challenge

Challenge these children to find out the meanings of the words 'tincture', 'curvature', 'posture', 'caricature' and 'horticulture'.

Homework / Additional activities

Spelling test

Ask the children to learn one of the following lists of words for a spelling test. Challenge them to write sentences for five of the words on their list.

Core words			Support words			Challenge words		
mixture	picture	puncture	mixture	nature	feature	mixture	future	furniture
departure	future	temperature	departure	picture	vulture	departure	creature	miniature
capture	creature	furniture	capture	future	puncture	capture	feature	moisture
adventure	feature	miniature	adventure	creature		adventure	vulture	structure
nature	vulture	moisture				nature	puncture	gesture
						picture	temperature	texture

Collins Connect: Unit 12

Ask the children to complete Unit 12 (see Teach → Year 4 → Spelling → Unit 12).

# Unit 13: The ending –sion

Overview

English curriculum objectives
- Endings which sound like /zhun/

Treasure House resources
- Spelling Skills Pupil Book 4, Unit 13, pages 30–31
- Collins Connect Treasure House Spelling Year 4, Unit 13
- Photocopiable Unit 13, Resource 1: Rainforest excursion, page 108
- Photocopiable Unit 13, Resource 2: A confusion of spellings, page 109

Additional resources
- Word cards: vision, division, television, explosion, decision, confusion, conclusion, occasion, invasion, illusion, revision, collision, diversion, excursion, erosion, version, action, condition, station, nation, condition, notion, information, frustration, temptation, optician, percussion, discussion
- Plain paper
- Glue sticks
- Use of computers

Introduction

Teaching overview
The buzzy /zhun/ sound at the end of words such as 'television' and 'explosion' is usually spelt '–sion'. Children need to be able hear the difference between this ending and the endings of words such as 'station' and 'nation' that end with /shun/. Not all words ending '–sion' are pronounced /zhun/ (see Unit 15) but almost all words pronounced /zhun/ are spelt '–sion'.

Introduce the concept
Say the words 'confusion' and 'pollution', emphasising the different sounds at the ends of the words. Ask: 'Do these words have the same sound at the end?' Agree that 'confusion' ends with a buzzy 'zhun' sound and 'pollution' with a softer /shun/ sound. Explain that the soft /shun/ sound can be spelt in a number of ways but the buzzy /zhun/ sound is always spelt '–sion'. Ask the children if they can think of any words that end /zhun/. Encourage them to remember the work they

did on this ending in Year 3. Write down the words the children suggest. Enhance the list, using the Challenge spelling list (see Spelling test) if needed, when they have exhausted their own ideas.

Reinforce the relationship between the /zhun/ ending and the '–sion' spelling. If the children suggest words that actually have a /shun/ ending, write these on the other side of the board and help the children to hear the difference. Reassure them that it is quite a subtle, though important, distinction.

Organise the children into groups and give each group a set of word cards (see Additional resources), a piece of plain paper and a glue stick. Tell them to sort the cards into words with a /zhun/ ending and words with a /shun/ ending, to stick them in two columns on their paper, to underline the ending of each word, to label their columns then to bring their sheet to the front of the class. Remind them to work as a team to complete the task, taking on different roles, sharing out the words, and so on.

Pupil practice
Pupil Book pages 30–31

Get started
The children correct misspelt words. Read the words together and ensure the children can hear the /zhun/ sound. Remind the children that this sound is always spelt '–sion'. Tell them to use this knowledge to correct the words. Discuss the meaning of 'illusion', 'division', 'version' and 'aversion'.

Answers
1. *revision*	[example]
2. illusion	[1 mark]
3. excursion	[1 mark]
4. confusion	[1 mark]
5. division	[1 mark]
6. version	[1 mark]
7. television	[1 mark]
8. aversion	[1 mark]

Try these
The children pair nouns ending '–sion' with the related verb. Ask the children to pair up the words. Clarify the meanings of 'invasion' and 'implosion'.

Answers
Noun	Verb	
conclusion	*conclude*	[example]
television	televise	[1 mark]
erosion	erode	[1 mark]

revision	revise	[1 mark]
diversion	divert	[1 mark]
explosion	explode	[1 mark]
implosion	implode	[1 mark]
invasion	invade	[1 mark]

Now try these

The children compose sentences using the target words 'television', 'diversion', 'invasion', 'explosion', 'erosion', 'diversion', 'conclusion' and 'occasion'.

Read the words together and ensure that the children understand the meaning of each. Tell the children to share their ideas with a partner before writing. Afterwards, share the children's sentences.

Answers

Aggie settled down to watch some television. [example]

Accept any sentences where the target word is correctly spelt and used. [8 marks: 1 mark per sentence]

Support, embed & challenge

Support

Use example words from the word cards (see Additional resources) to ensure that all the children can hear the difference between the /zhun/ and the /shun/ endings. Read out each word in turn and ask the children to raise a hand if they can hear the /zhun/ ending. Help the children make a connection between the buzzy /zh/ sound in 'measure', 'treasure' and 'leisure' and the same sound in words ending /zhun/.

Ask the children to complete Unit 13 Resource 1: Rainforest excursion. Afterwards, read the words from the story to the children and ask them to write down the last four letters of each word as you read them. Once the last letters are written, work together to write each complete word. (**Answers** erosion, excursion, diversion, television, explosion, collision, enclosure)

Repeat the 'Try these' activity in the Pupil Book on a computer. Some children might find using the delete button to delete errors a helpful reminder of the process.

Embed

The collection of words for this unit would work well in an adventure story: 'erosion', 'explosion', 'confusion', 'collision', 'decision', 'diversion', 'invasion'. Challenge the children to write their own mini-adventure, either as a storyboard with captions or as paragraphs of text. Perhaps an alien invasion could lead to an explosion. Severe rain could cause erosion and landslides which could result in diversions. Chaos and confusion and difficult decisions could abound for the hero …

Read out the word cards (see Additional resources) one last time. Ask the children to stand up when they hear a word with a /zhun/ ending and sit down when they hear a word with a /shun/ ending.

Ask the children to complete Unit 13 Resource 2: A confusion of spellings. (**Answers** 1. explosion, 2. diversion, 3. confusion, 4. invasion, 5. conclusion, 6. illusion, 7. television, 8. occasion)

Challenge

Challenge these children to write a longer adventure story, adding in as many words from their spelling list (see Spelling test) as possible.

Ask these children to investigate the meanings of the words 'aversion', 'erosion', 'diversion' and 'intrusion'.

Homework / Additional activities

Spelling test

Ask the children to learn one of the following lists of words for a spelling test. Challenge them to write sentences for five of the words on their list.

Core words			Support words			Challenge words		
vision	conclusion	revision	vision	decision	occasion	vision	confusion	provision
division	confusion	collision	division	conclusion	invasion	division	occasion	version
television	occasion	provision	television	confusion	illusion	television	invasion	erosion
explosion	invasion	version	explosion			explosion	illusion	excursion
decision	illusion					decision	revision	implosion
						conclusion	collision	

Collins Connect: Unit 13

Ask the children to complete Unit 13 (see Teach → Year 4 → Spelling → Unit 13).

Unit 14: The suffix –ous

Overview

English curriculum objectives
- The suffix –ous

Treasure House resources
- Spelling Skills Pupil Book 4, Unit 14, pages 32–33
- Collins Connect Treasure House Spelling Year 4, Unit 14
- Photocopiable Unit 14, Resource 1: Ser<u>ious</u> spellings, page 110
- Photocopiable Unit 14, Resource 2: Marvell<u>ous</u> –<u>ous</u> words, page 111

Additional resources
- Word cards: furious, marvellous, anxious, glorious, dangerous, hazardous, disastrous, ridiculous, suspicious, poisonous, ambitious, numerous, glamorous, nervous, serious, various, curious, dangerous, enormous, fabulous, famous, furious, generous, mysterious, adventurous, mountainous, prosperous, famous, advantageous, courageous, outrageous, mysterious, gorgeous

Introduction

Teaching overview
The /us/ ending at the end of many adjectives is spelt '–ous'. There are hundreds of words ending '–ous' and the rules for adding '–ous' to root words are rather complicated:

1. For many words, just add '–ous', for example, 'hazard' → 'hazardous'.
2. For words ending 'e', usually drop the 'e', for example, 'fame' → 'famous'.
3. For words ending /j/ ('ge'), keep the final 'e', for example, 'advantage' → 'advantageous'. There are very few of these words.
4. For words ending 'y', change the 'y' to an 'i', for example, 'vary' → 'various'.
5. For words ending 'our', change 'our' to 'or', for example, 'glamour' → 'glamorous'.
6. Many words have no clear root word, such as 'serious' and 'obvious'. When there is an /ee/ sound before the /us/, the '–ious' ending is more common than the '–eous' ending. But there are still quite a few words ending '–eous', such as 'gorgeous' and 'miscellaneous'.

Introduce the concept
Introduce the /us/ sound spelt '–ous'. Create a chart on the board for rules 1 to 5, plus a column for 'no clear root', writing an example in each column. Give each child a word card (see Additional resources) and ask them to turn to a partner and read the word. Together, they should decide if any part of the word is difficult to spell, identify what the root word might have been and work out which column their word should go in. Ask for volunteers to read out their words and to test you on your spelling. Model applying the spelling rules and write each word in the appropriate column. For each word, ask the children if that was the column they thought it should go in.

Once you have demonstrated each spelling rule a few times, ask any children whose words have not been covered yet to come to the front and to copy their words into the correct column of the table on the board. Read all the words together.

Pupil practice

Pupil Book pages 32–33

Get started
The children identify and write the root words of adjectives. Discuss the meanings of 'vigorous', 'prosperous' and 'hazardous', using the root word as part of your explanation. Explain that they may need to add (or reorder) letters to recreate the original root word. Afterwards, discuss how 'miracle' became 'miraculous', 'envy' became 'envious', and 'humour' became 'humorous'. Discuss the meaning of 'vigour', 'prosper' and 'hazard'.

Answers
1. *ridicule*		*[example]*
2. humour		[1 mark]
3. miracle		[1 mark]
4. envy		[1 mark]
5. vigour		[1 mark]
6. prosper		[1 mark]
7. hazard		[1 mark]
8. fame		[1 mark]

Try these

The children identify and correct the spelling mistakes in words. Discuss the meanings of any unfamiliar words, such as 'spontaneous'. Remind them to look at the spelling rules for adding the suffix '–ous' on the previous page of the Pupil Book. Also, point out that they might find some of the words written elsewhere on the page of the Pupil Book, for example in the introduction or one of the other activities. Afterwards, clarify the correct spellings, making connections with the rules. Point out the /sh/ sound spelt 'ci' in 'spacious'.

Answers

1. *adventurous*	*[example]*
2. spontaneous	[1 mark]
3. spacious	[1 mark]
4. jealous	[1 mark]
5. numerous	[1 mark]
6. humorous	[1 mark]
7. outrageous	[1 mark]
8. mischievous	[1 mark]

Now try these

The children compose sentences using the target words 'famous', 'nauseous', 'contagious', 'obvious', 'generous', 'momentous', 'mischievous' and 'anonymous'. Read the words together and ensure that the children understand the meaning of each. Afterwards, share the children's sentences.

Answers

Adjay's virus was <u>contagious</u>, so the doctor told him to stay in bed.   *[example]*

Accept any sentences where the target word is correctly spelt and used. [8 marks: 1 mark per sentence]

Support, embed & challenge

Support

Focus with these children on creating a clear link in their minds between the /us/ sound and the '–ous' ending. Use the most useful and straightforward words to achieve this, such as 'famous', 'dangerous', 'serious', 'enormous' and 'generous'. Use the word cards (see Additional resources) to read through the words with these children, focus on the '–ous' endings and have them copy each word a few times onto their whiteboards.

Ask the children to complete Unit 14 Resource 1: Ser<u>ious</u> spellings. (**Answers** For each question, accept any adjective from the list that is correctly spelt and appropriate to the context.)

Afterwards, provide them with a second copy of the resource sheet and ask them to carry out the activity again, choosing a different adjective for each picture this time. As a group, make up new noun phrases for each of the adjectives on the sheet. Scribe these for the group, modelling the spelling rules as you write each '–ous' word.

Embed

Provide the children with the images and word bank on Unit 14 Resource 1 Ser<u>ious</u> spellings, and ask them to write a noun phrase of their own under each image.

Discuss the spellings of '–ous' words with the children. Agree that it is probably the trickiest spelling pattern to learn so far because there are so many rules and exceptions. Share the bad news that many of the words just have to be learned, but encourage them with the good news that they are fabulous words to use in any adventurous and marvellous descriptive writing they might want to do.

Ask the children to use Unit 14 Resource 2: Marvell<u>ous</u> –ous words, using multiple copies if necessary, to practise spelling these treacherous words.

Challenge

These adjectives lend themselves to descriptive writing. Ask these children to write a descriptive paragraph using as many of the adjectives as possible. For example, they could write about a glamorous film star arriving at a fabulous party, or a dangerous trip along a hazardous path up a mountainous road. Provide them with the images from Unit 14 Resource to inspire them if it helps.

Homework / Additional activities

Spelling test

Ask the children to learn one of the following lists of words for a spelling test. Challenge them to write sentences for five of the words on their list.

Core words		Support words		Challenge words	
serious	generous	serious	fabulous	serious	marvellous
various	marvellous	various	famous	various	cautious
curious	cautious	curious	furious	curious	jealous
dangerous	jealous	dangerous	generous	dangerous	delicious
enormous	delicious	enormous	marvellous	enormous	mysterious
fabulous	mysterious			fabulous	disastrous
famous	disastrous			famous	anxious
furious				furious	glamorous
				generous	suspicious

Collins Connect: Unit 14

Ask the children to complete Unit 14 (see Teach → Year 4 → Spelling → Unit 14).

Unit 15: The endings –tion, –sion, –ssion and –cian

Overview

English curriculum objectives

- Endings which sound like /shun/ spelt –tion, –sion, –ssion, –cian

Treasure House resources

- Spelling Skills Pupil Book 4, Unit 15, pages 34–35
- Collins Connect Treasure House Spelling Year 4, Unit 15
- Photocopiable Unit 15, Resource 1: /shun/ collections, page 112

- Photocopiable Unit 15, Resource 2: Your mission: Learn these spellings, page 113

Additional resources

- Word cards: perfection, population, invention, mention, information, action, election, eruption, hesitation, education, information, question, direction, discussion, permission, percussion, discussion, expression, admission, confession, optician, mathematician, musician, technician, expansion, extension, comprehension, tension, revulsion
- Glue sticks

Introduction

Teaching overview

This is another tricky set of words to learn. The /shun/ sound at the end of words is spelt '–tion', '–sion', '–ssion' or '–cian'. Of these, the '–tion' ending is the most common. When deciding which ending to use, an associated root word can provide a useful clue, for example, 'invent' → 'invention', 'tense' → 'tension','discuss' → 'discussion', 'music' → 'musician'. Words ending '–cian' are often jobs, for example, 'physician' and 'optician'.

Introduce the concept

Give a word card to each child. Ask the children to work in groups to look at their cards and work out what spelling pattern you are practising this week. Agree that it is the /shun/ ending. Ask the groups to use their cards, and their prior knowledge, to have a go at defining the rules for spelling this ending. Ask

volunteers from each group to suggest endings and rules and use this information to gradually fill in a chart on the board with a column for each ending and the rules, with examples, in each column. Ask the children to decide if their word has an identifiable root word and, if so, what they think it is. Encourage them to discuss their ideas in their groups. Clarify the key points, asking the children to put their hand up if their word fits one of these rules.

- Words ending '–cian' are types of workers.
- Some words have no root.
- Root words ending 'd' take '–sion'.
- Root words ending 't' take '–ssion'.
- Root words ending 'e' lose the 'e'.

Ask the children to come to the front and to write their word in the correct column of the table. Read the words together.

Pupil practice

Pupil Book pages 34–35

Get started

The children identify and write the correct spellings of words that end /shun/. Afterwards, ask them to underline the spelling of the /shun/ sound in each word. Ask the children to point out the different spelling patterns.

Answers

1. *temptation*	*[example]*
2. completion	[1 mark]
3. beautician	[1 mark]
4. examination	[1 mark]
5. tension	[1 mark]

Try these

The children add the /shun/ ending to root words. Tell them to keep checking the rules on the previous page (for example, with '–mit' remove the 't' and add '–ssion').

Answers

1. *confession*	*[example]*
2. pollution	[1 mark]
3. exception	[1 mark]
4. electrician	[1 mark]
5. admission	[1 mark]
6. comprehension	[1 mark]
7. mathematician	[1 mark]
8. submission	[1 mark]

Now try these

The children compose sentences using the target words 'vacation', 'fiction', 'mission', 'immersion', 'expansion', 'fraction', 'obsession' and 'musician'. Read the words together and ensure that the children understand the meaning of each. Tell the children to share their ideas with a partner before writing. Afterwards, share the children's sentences.

Answers

This year we went camping for our vacation. [example]

Accept any sentences where the target word is correctly spelt and used. [8 marks: 1 mark per sentence]

Support, embed & challenge

Support

Create an enlarged A3 version of Unit 15 Resource 1: /shun/ collections. Organise these children into groups of four. Cut out the words and put them in the centre of each group. Give each child one of the endings to master and ask him or her to find the words and underline the endings. Together, stick the words in the correct column and read them. Discuss the meanings of any unknown words.

Ask the children to complete their own copy of Unit 15 Resource 1, writing the words if possible. If necessary, reduce the number of words for sorting by blanking out a few before photocopying. (**Answers** spelt '–tion': action, attention, collection, direction, education, information, introduction, competition, mention; spelt '–sion': extension, mansion, expansion, version, tension; spelt '–ssion': permission, passion, percussion, possession, obsession, discussion, admission, impression; spelt '–cian': electrician, mathematician, physician, politician, technician, beautician, musician, optician; the words ending '–cian' are all professions; the column for words ending '–tion' has the most words)

Embed

Ask the children to complete Unit 15 Resource 2: Your mission: Learn these spellings. (**Answers** association, mathematician, attention, musician, extension, expression, education, physician, competition, admission, invention, permission, impression, opposition, politician, electrician, injection, obsession, expansion, permission, submission)

Ask the children to work in pairs and give each pair a set of word cards (see Additional resources) or a set of the words from Unit 15 Resource 1, if you prefer. Tell them to read the words together, discussing the endings and how they can remember them. Remind the children that, if they can identify the root word, it might give them a clue to which ending to use. Ask the children to take turns selecting a card and reading the word for their partner to spell on their whiteboard.

Challenge

Ask these children to work in a group. Allocate a word ending /shun/ and its definition to each child. Allocate words that they are unlikely to know, such as, 'denomination', 'cessation', 'fabrication', 'demarcation', 'conscription'. Ask these children to write the definition of the word they have been allocated along with two other fake definitions for the word. Tell them to read their word and the three definitions to the group and ask the others to guess which definition is the correct one.

Homework / Additional activities

Spelling test

Ask the children to learn one of the following lists of words for a spelling test. Challenge them to write sentences for five of the words on their list.

Core words		Support words		Challenge words	
relation	musician	relation	direction	connection	expression
solution	expression	solution	education	distinction	percussion
direction	percussion	station	information	definition	permission
education	permission	action	musician	investigation	impression
position	possession	question		contribution	obsession
eruption	expansion			consideration	extension
attention	tension			exhibition	version
				mathematician	expansion
				technician	tension

Collins Connect: Unit 15

Ask the children to complete Unit 15 (see Teach → Year 4 → Spelling → Unit 15).

Unit 16: The /k/ sound spelt ch

Overview

English curriculum objectives
- Words with the /k/ sound spelt ch (Greek in origin)

Treasure House resources
- Spelling Skills Pupil Book 4, Unit 16, pages 36–37
- Collins Connect Treasure House Spelling Year 4, Unit 16
- Photocopiable Unit 16, Resource 1: Spellings to make your head a<u>ch</u>e, page 114

- Photocopiable Unit 16, Resource 2: A s<u>ch</u>ooling in /k/ spelt <u>ch</u>, page 115

Additional resources
Word cards: ache, anchor, archaeology, architect, chaos, character, chasm, chemist, chemistry, choir, cholera, chord, chorus, echo, headache, mechanic, monarch, orchestra, scheme, school, stomach, technical, technology, orchid, heartache, mechanism, chaotic, echoing, monarchy, technician

Introduction

Teaching overview
There are a number of words that spell the /k/ sound 'ch'. Of these, the most useful are 'school', 'stomach', 'chorus', 'character', 'choir', 'scheme' and 'headache'. These words just need to be learned.

Introduce the concept
At a time when the children cannot see what you are doing, hide the word cards (see Additional resources) around the classroom. Organise the children into groups. Tell them to search the classroom for the word cards, taking each card they find back to their group. The group who finds the most cards wins.

Ask the groups to read through the words they have found. Ask the group with the most cards to read the words out. Ask: 'What spelling pattern are we practising today?' Confirm that is /k/ spelt 'ch'. Ask each group to swap cards with another group and then read and discuss the new words. Have the groups keep swapping cards until each group has read each set. Collect the cards and ask the children to work in their groups to write down as many words with /k/ spelt 'ch' as they can remember. Award a point for each correctly spelt word. Award bonus points for any words remembered by only one group. Compile a list of all the words and display it.

Pupil practice

Pupil Book pages 36–37

Get started
The children sort the words into two groups: words where the /k/ sound is spelt 'ch' and words where it is not. Read each word together ensuring the children are confident with them. Clarify the meaning of 'monarch', 'anchor' and 'chemistry'.

Answers

The /k/ sound spelt 'ch'		The /k/ sound not spelt 'ch'	
monarch	[example]	skunk	[1 mark]
anchor	[1 mark]	kite	[1 mark]
chemistry	[1 mark]	cake	[1 mark]
character	[1 mark]	seek	[1 mark]

Try these
The children complete words with the letters 'ch' or 'c'. Before they do so, explain to the children that the missing sound in each word is the /k/ sound.

Answers
1. *chaos*	*[example]*
2. cook	[1 mark]
3. orchestra	[1 mark]
4. Scotland	[1 mark]
5. technology	[1 mark]
6. echo	[1 mark]
7. scary	[1 mark]
8. stomach	[1 mark]

Now try these
The children correct the spellings of words and then use them in sentences of their own. Ask the children to read the words phonetically, before deciding how they need to be corrected. Tell them to share their ideas with a partner before writing their sentences. Afterwards, share the children's sentences.

Answers

1. *Charlie strummed a <u>chord</u> on her guitar.* *[example]*
2. chemist [1 mark]
3. chemistry [1 mark]
4. anchor [1 mark]

5. chaos [1 mark]
6. scheme [1 mark]
7. technical [1 mark]

Accept any sentences where the target word is correctly spelt and used. [6 marks: 1 mark per sentence]

Support, embed & challenge

Support

Reread the word cards (see Additional resources) with this group, focussing on those words that match their ability level. Write a list of words, including those from the word cards plus other words with the /k/ sound spelt 'k', 'c' or 'ck', such as 'bank', 'kitten', 'pick', 'fake', 'freak', 'cream', 'stack' and 'bike'. Leave a gap in each word for the letter or letters that stand for /k/ and encourage the children to suggest what to fill the gaps with.

Ask the children to complete Unit 16 Resource 1 Spellings to make your head a<u>ch</u>e, which challenges the children to find words that use 'ch' for /k/. (**Answers** colour ed in: school, headache, scheme, orchestra, chemistry, echo, anchor, chorus, mechanic, character, choir, chaos, ache, stomach, chasm)

Embed

The key to mastering this spelling pattern is simply learning the list of words. Ask the children to work in pairs and provide the pairs with a list of the words on the word cards (see Additional resources). Challenge them to take turns to remember as many words as possible while their partner ticks them off on the list. Once they have remembered all the words on the list, tell the children to use words from their list to play a game of 'Hangman' with their partner.

Ask the children to complete Unit 16 Resource 2: A s<u>ch</u>ooling in /k/ spelt <u>ch</u>. (**Answers** 1. anchor, 2. choir, 3. orchestra, 4. headache, 5. school, 6. chasm, 7. echoes, 8. mechanic, 9. character, 10. chemist, chemistry, 11. character, scheme, 12. stomach, ache)

Challenge

Ask these children to write a 100-word description of, or story about, a chaotic event in a school chemistry lab. They should try to use as many words from the class list as possible.

Homework / Additional activities

Spelling test

Ask the children to learn one of the following lists of words for a spelling test. Challenge them to write sentences for five of the words on their list.

Core words		Support words		Challenge words	
anchor	headache	anchor	chasm	anchor	character
chaos	character	chaos	scheme	chaos	mechanic
choir	mechanic	choir	school	choir	technical
chorus	technical	chorus	headache	chorus	technician
echo	technician	echo	character	echo	chord
chasm	chord			chasm	monarch
scheme	monarch			scheme	chemist
school				school	archaeology
				headache	orchid

Collins Connect: Unit 16

Ask the children to complete Unit 16 (see Teach → Year 4 → Spelling → Unit 16).

Unit 17: The /sh/ sound spelt ch

Overview

English curriculum objectives
- Words with the /sh/ sound spelt ch (mostly French in origin)

Treasure House resources
- Spelling Skills Pupil Book 4, Unit 17, pages 38–39
- Collins Connect Treasure House Spelling Year 4, Unit 17
- Photocopiable Unit 17, Resource 1: /sh/ spelt <u>ch</u> letter match, page 116

- Photocopiable Unit 17, Resource 2: A ni<u>ch</u>e spelling pattern, page 117

Additional resources
- Word cards: moustache, chef, machine, parachute, charade, machete, quiche, sachet, chalet, brochure, chandelier, chic, chicane, chateau, chauffeur, chaperone, chute, niche
- Bags to draw letters from (for Resource 1)
- Yellow, blue and green colouring pencils or highlighters (for Resource 2)

Introduction

Teaching overview

Although children need to be aware of the /sh/ sound spelt 'ch', most of the words with this spelling are not very useful for Year 4 children, with the exceptions of 'machine' and 'chef' and perhaps 'moustache'. Being able to spell names such as 'Michelle' and 'Charlotte' could also be useful if the children know anyone by these names. Other words that can be used to practise this spelling are 'quiche', 'chalet', 'brochure', 'chandelier', 'parachute', 'charade', 'machete' and 'sachet'.

Introduce the concept

Organise the children into groups and deal out the word cards (see Additional resources) equally between each group. Ask the children to read their words and suggest what spelling pattern they are about to practise. Share the words and recap on the spelling pattern. Ensure that the children understand all the words on the cards they have. Explain that most of these words have come from France. Challenge the children to work in their groups to

make up a sentence using two or three of their words. Swap cards between groups, or hand out more cards if the children find their selection limiting. Share the sentences, writing them on the board, along with suggestions of your own, for example:

'The chef served the quiche with a twirl of his moustache.'

'Michelle Montgomery-Jones nonchalantly parachuted down to her chateau.'

'Charlotte dropped a stitch in her crochet when her chauffeur took the chicane too fast.'

'Chic Charlene found a niche under the chandelier to sit and sip some tea and flick through the brochures.'

'The ball ricocheted off the chandelier and landed in the coffee machine.'

'The children played charades whilst their chaperone ate chips with a sachet of ketchup.'

Ask the children to write down their favourite sentences to help them associate words with similar spelling patterns.

Pupil practice

Pupil Book pages 38–39

Get started

The children correct spelling mistakes in words. Ask the children to replace each 'sh' with 'ch'. Once they have written the new words, read the words together and ask the children to discuss meanings of in a group the words. Share the ideas and ask motoring fans to explain what a 'chicane' is (a double bend).

Answers

1. *chefs*		*[example]*
2. chicane		[1 mark]
3. chateau		[1 mark]
4. quiche		[1 mark]
5. chauffeur		[1 mark]
6. crochet		[1 mark]
7. sachet		[1 mark]
8. chaperone		[1 mark]

Try these

The children rearrange jumbled letters to spell words with the /sh/ sound spelt 'ch'. Remind them of the focus of the unit. Suggest they put the 'ch' letters together first and then see if the rest of the letters suggest a word they know.

Answers

1. *chute*	*[example]*
2. moustache	[1 mark]
3. machine	[1 mark]
4. chandelier	[1 mark]
5. chalet	[1 mark]
6. parachute	[1 mark]
7. quiche	[1 mark]
8. niche	[1 mark]

Now try these

The children compose sentences using the target words 'machines', 'brochure', 'chandelier', 'parachute', 'chauffeur', 'quiche', 'nonchalant', 'ricochet.' Read the words together and ensure that the children understand the meaning of each. Tell the children to share their ideas with a partner before writing. Afterwards, share the children's sentences.

Answers

Computers are very useful <u>machines</u>.   *[example]*

Accept any sentences where the target word is correctly spelt and used. [8 marks: 1 mark per sentence]

Support, embed & challenge

Support

Reread the word cards (see Additional resources). Provide the children with two words each from Unit 17 Resource 1: /sh/ spelt <u>ch</u> letter match. Read the eight words together and agree on the sounds in the words. Play the game a couple of times so that the children play with most of the words.

Cut out the words from Unit 17 Resource 2: A ni<u>ch</u>e spelling pattern, and work with the children to sort these into three sets: words where 'ch' spells /k/, words where 'ch' spells /sh/ and words where 'ch' spells /ch/.

Focus on practising the spellings of the key words that are most useful for these children: 'machine', 'chef', 'parachute' and 'sachet'.

Embed

Ask the children to return to the sentences with words where 'ch' spells /sh/ that they wrote previously. Give the children some time to memorise them. Display a complete list of the words from the word cards on the board and ask the children to write more sentences using whichever words they feel are most useful to them. (The words 'chateau' and 'chauffeur' have multiple tricky spelling patterns so you may wish to leave them out for now.)

Ask the children to complete Unit 17 Resource 2: A ni<u>ch</u>e spelling pattern. (**Answers** yellow: school, headache, scheme, orchestra, chemistry, chaotic, echo, anchor, chorus, mechanic, character, choir, chaos, ache, stomach, chasm; blue: chef, chalet, chateau, machine, charade, parachute, niche, pistachio, sachet, chute, moustache, quiche, chandelier; green: cheers, chicken, touch, bleach, watch, searching, chalk, chip, cheese, each, crunching, champion, pinches, archer, punched, match)

Tell the children to check each other's coloured in sheets. Tell the children to write out the words on their resource sheet as three separate lists: words where 'ch' spells /k/, words where 'ch' spells /sh/ and words where 'ch' spells /ch/.

Challenge

Ask these children to create a short story opener (perhaps about a chic model who is driven to her chateau by her chauffeur) using as many words as possible with this spelling pattern.

Homework / Additional activities

Spelling test

Ask the children to learn one of the following lists of words for a spelling test. Challenge them to write sentences for five of the words on their list.

Core words		Support words		Challenge words	
moustache	sachet	chef	machete	moustache	brochure
chef	chalet	moustache	quiche	chef	chandelier
machine	brochure	machine	sachet	machine	chic
parachute	chic	parachute	chalet	parachute	chicane
charade	chute	charade	brochure	charade	chateau
machete	niche			machete	chauffeur
quiche				quiche	chaperone
				sachet	chute
				chalet	niche

Collins Connect: Unit 17

Ask the children to complete Unit 17 (see Teach → Year 4 → Spelling → Unit 17).

Review unit 2

Pupil Book pages 40–41

A. Ask the children to choose the correct spelling of each word.

1. sachet [1 mark]

2. machine [1 mark]

3. chorus [1 mark]

4. pollution [1 mark]

5. admission [1 mark]

6. spacious [1 mark]

7. ridiculous [1 mark]

8. conclusion [1 mark]

9. feature [1 mark]

10. measure [1 mark]

11. sensation [1 mark]

B. Ask the children to add the suffixes to the words. Remind them that they might need to change the ending of the original word before they add the suffix.

1. accusation [1 mark]

2. obligation [1 mark]

3. preparation [1 mark]

4. terribly [1 mark]

5. crumbly [1 mark]

6. crazily [1 mark]

7. humorous [1 mark]

8. admission [1 mark]

C. Ask the children to complete and write down the missing word from each of the sentences.

1. spontaneous [1 mark]

2. condensation [1 mark]

3. greedily [1 mark]

4. leisure [1 mark]

5. adventure [1 mark]

6. illusion [1 mark]

7. Miraculously [1 mark]

8. permission [1 mark]

9. anchor [1 mark]

Unit 18: The /k/ sound spelt –que and the /g/ sound spelt –gue

Overview

English curriculum objectives
- Words ending with the /g/ sound spelt –gue and the /k/ sound spelt –que (French in origin)

Treasure House resources
- Spelling Skills Pupil Book 4, Unit 18, pages 42–43
- Collins Connect Treasure House Spelling Year 4, Unit 18
- Photocopiable Unit 18, Resource 1: Conquer these grotesque spellings, page 118

- Photocopiable Unit 18, Resource 2: A crossword of intrigue, page 119

Additional resources
- Word cards: tongue, rogue, league, meringue, catalogue, vague, fatigue, plague, intrigue, dialogue, colleague, antique, conquered, cheque, unique, grotesque, technique, physique, opaque, boutique

Introduction

Teaching overview

In some words, the /g/ sound at the ends of words is spelt '–gue', for example, 'league', 'tongue', 'rogue', 'vague', 'meringue' and 'catalogue'. In some words, the /k/ sound is spelt '–que' at the ends of words, for example, 'antique', 'cheque', 'unique' and 'grotesque'. These words are not generally very useful for Year 4 children but the children do need to be aware of the spelling patterns. The words 'quiche' and 'queue' also have the 'que' for /k/ spelling pattern, but at the beginning of the word rather than the end.

Introduce the concept

Write the words 'plague' and 'plaque' on the board. Ask the children to turn to a partner and decide how each word is pronounced and what each word means. Share the children's ideas and agree on the pronunciation and definition of each. Ask volunteers

to come to the front, underline the endings and say what sound each ending represents: /g/ for '–gue' and /k/ for '–que'. Hand out the word cards (see Additional resources). Ask the children to read the word you have given them and determine its pronunciation and meaning. Encourage the children to ask for help from classmates or yourself if they do not know. Point out that many of the words are quite obscure so you would be surprised if no one needed help.

Ask the children to stand up if they have a word ending '–gue'. Ask each child to read out their word and say what it means. Clarify the meanings of new words, providing exemplar sentences. Ask each child to write their word on the board under a '–gue' heading. Ask the children with words ending '–que' to stand, say their word and its definition and then write it on the board under a '–que' heading.

Pupil practice

Pupil Book pages 42–43

Get started

The children correct spelling mistakes in words. Explain that each of these words has the wrong ending. Ask them to rewrite the words with the correct ending. Afterwards, read the words together clarifying the meanings of 'boutique' and 'fatigue'.

Answers
1. *boutique*	*[example]*
2. antique	[1 mark]
3. catalogue	[1 mark]
4. vague	[1 mark]
5. fatigue	[1 mark]
6. grotesque	[1 mark]
7. tongue	[1 mark]
8. meringue	[1 mark]

Try these

The children copy and complete sentences with words ending '–gue' and '–que'. Ask the children to read the words in the box and discuss the meaning and pronunciation of each with a partner. Tell them to match the words to the sentences, writing out the sentences in full.

Answers

1. *My <u>colleague</u> was on holiday last week.*   *[example]*
2. The athlete trained hard to keep his <u>physique</u> in good shape.   [1 mark]
3. The plot of his latest story was full of mystery and <u>intrigue</u>.   [1 mark]
4. Many of the villagers were struck down with the <u>plague</u> and died.   [1 mark]
5. The windows in the room were made of <u>opaque</u> glass.   [1 mark]

Now try these

The children compose sentences using the target words 'league', 'dialogue', 'intrigue', 'boutique', 'grotesque', 'rogue', 'colleague' and 'opaque'. Read the words together and ensure that the children understand the meaning of each, particularly 'intrigue' and 'opaque'. Tell the children to share their ideas with a partner before writing. Afterwards, share the children's sentences.

Answers

One day, John and Casper hoped to play in the big <u>league</u>.   *[example]*

Accept any sentences where the target word is correctly spelt and used. [8 marks: 1 mark per sentence]

Support, embed & challenge

Support

Read the word cards (see Additional resources) together, emphasising the /g/ and /k/ endings. Discuss the meaning of each word. Shuffle the cards and hold them out face down in a fan. Ask each child, in turn, to take one card and read it out. Ask the rest of the group to write /k/ or /g/ on their whiteboard. Continue until the children are familiar with all the words and are confident with both the endings.

Ask the children to complete Unit 18 Resource 1: Conquer these grotesque spellings. Afterwards, read all the words together sounding out the phonemes and clarifying the meanings. (**Answers** conquered, catalogue, unique, rogue, grotesque, league, plague and plaque, opaque, meringue, vague, intrigue, dialogue, tongue, antique, technique)

Embed

Organise the children into groups and provide each group with a set of word cards (see Additional resources). Ask them to spread the cards out, read the cards together as a group and spend some time helping each other to learn the spellings. Tell the children to shuffle the word cards and place them face down in a pile in the middle of the group. Ask them to take turns to pick up a card and ask the child on their left to spell the word on it. If the child spells the word correctly, they may keep the card, displaying it in front of them. If not, the card goes to the bottom of the pile. The children should continue until all the cards are gone. The winner is the child with the most cards.

Ask the children to complete Unit 18 Resource 2: A crossword of intrigue. (**Answers** Across: 3. vague, 4. dialogue, 6. tongue, 9. intrigue, 10. league; Down: 1. opaque, 2. plaque, 5. grotesque, 7. antique, 8. unique)

Challenge

Challenge these children to write a series of silly sentences for '–gue' and '–que' words. Each sentence should have either three '–que' words (for example, 'The antique dealer said the opaque paperweight was unique.') or three '–gue' words (for example, 'The meringue stuck to my tongue and made dialogue difficult.'). Afterwards, ask them to share their sentences with the rest of the class, encouraging the other children to learn the sentences to aid their memory of the spelling pattern.

Homework / Additional activities

Spelling test

Ask the children to learn one of the following lists of words for a spelling test. Challenge them to write sentences for five of the words on their list.

Core words		Support words		Challenge words	
tongue	antique	tongue	antique	tongue	antique
rogue	conquered	rogue	unique	rogue	conquered
league	unique	league	grotesque	league	cheque
meringue	grotesque	vague	opaque	meringue	unique
catalogue	technique	intrigue		catalogue	grotesque
vague	opaque	dialogue		vague	technique
plague				plague	opaque
intrigue				intrigue	boutique
dialogue				dialogue	
				colleague	

Collins Connect: Unit 18

Ask the children to complete Unit 18 (see Teach → Year 4 → Spelling → Unit 18).

# Unit 19: The /s/ sound spelt sc

Overview

English curriculum objectives
- Words with the /s/ sound spelt sc (Latin in origin)

Treasure House resources
- Spelling Skills Pupil Book 4, Unit 19, pages 44–45
- Collins Connect Treasure House Spelling Year 4, Unit 19
- Photocopiable Unit 19, Resource 1: Fascinating spellings, page 120

- Photocopiable Unit 19, Resource 2: Scenic spellings, page 121

Additional resources
- Word cards: scene, scissors, muscles, crescent, scab, biscuit, scary, cascade
- *Scrabble* tile or letter card sets to spell the words 'scene', 'scissors', 'muscles' and 'crescent'
- Blank cards for the children to create word cards
- Materials to make posters

Introduction

Teaching overview

The /s/ sound is spelt 'sc' in some words: 'scene', 'scent', 'science', 'scissors', 'crescent', 'descend', 'science', 'muscles'. The most useful of these words is 'scissors'.

Introduce the concept

Ask a volunteer to say a word with a /s/ sound, for example, 'silly'. Ask the children to write the word on their whiteboards and hold up the word. Discuss the spelling of the /s/ sound and write it as a heading (for example, /s/ spelt 's' or /s/ spelt 'ss'), writing the word underneath. Repeat with more words, creating new columns as the spelling patterns come up. After

a while, ask the children to write a few words with /s/ spelt 'c', such as 'city' and 'lace', if this spelling has not come up so far. Add a column for these words. Finally, ask them to have a go at writing the words 'crescent' and 'scissors' (if the /s/ spelt 'sc' spelling has not come up already), adding these in a final column. Recap on the spelling pattern and ask if anyone can remember other words with this spelling. Write these on the board then complete the list with 'scene', 'scent', 'science', 'ascent', 'descend', 'muscles', 'scenery', 'scenic' and 'fascinate'.

If appropriate for your children, introduce the words 'scythe' and 'adolescent' and explain to the class what these words mean.

Pupil practice

Pupil Book pages 44–45

Get started

The children complete words with the letters 's' or 'sc'. Look at the words together, clarifying what each is. Explain that each word can be completed with 's' or 'sc' and they need to choose which. Afterwards, sort the words into the different spelling patterns on the board.

Answers
1. *cases* — [example]
2. scene — [1 mark]
3. descend — [1 mark]
4. lost — [1 mark]
5. scenery — [1 mark]
6. citrus — [1 mark]
7. science — [1 mark]
8. social — [1 mark]

Try these

The children identify and correct spelling mistakes in misspelt words. Remind the children that the /s/ sound can be spelt 's', 'sc' or 'c'.

Answers
1. *scenic* — [example]
2. crescent — [1 mark]
3. descent — [1 mark]
4. sensible — [1 mark]
5. balance — [1 mark]
6. solid — [1 mark]

Now try these

The children compose sentences using the target words 'scissors', 'discipline', 'descend', 'adolescent', 'fascinate', 'ascend' and 'scent'. Read the words together and ensure that the children understand the meaning of each. Afterwards, share the children's sentences.

Answers

Emily used the sharp <u>scissors</u> to cut the paper shapes.   *[example]*

Accept any sentences where the target word is correctly spelt and used. [7 marks: 1 mark per sentence]

Support, embed & challenge

Support

Ask these children to carry out Unit 19 Resource 1: Fa<u>sc</u>inating <u>s</u>pellings. Afterwards, share the lists, underlining the /s/ spelling in each. (**Answers** /s/ spelt 'ss': scissors, bossy, princess, fussy, pressed; /s/ spelt 'c': lace, city, princess, bicycle, pencil, centre, fancy, sentence; /s/ spelt 's': snow, creases, lost, silent, scissors, books, pasta, festival, sentence, muscles; /s/ spelt 'sc': scent, crescent, fascinating, scissors, scene, muscles)

Provide these children with word cards of the most useful words: 'scene', 'scissors', 'muscles' and 'crescent' (see Additional resources). Ask the children to write each word drawing a line between each grapheme, for example, 'm/u/sc/l/e/s/'. Play a game of 'Hangman' using only these four words until they are confident of the spellings. Use *Scrabble* tiles (or letter cards), giving each child a set for each word and ask them to recreate the words.

Provide word cards for the words 'scab', 'biscuit', 'scary' and 'cascade' (see Additional resources). Read these together and discuss the sound the 'sc' spelling stands for in these words. Shuffle these cards in with the cards for 'scene', 'scissors', 'muscles' and 'crescent'. Hold up different words and ask the children to say /s/ or /sc/ depending on the sound.

Embed

Ask the children to create word cards for 'muscles', 'scissors', 'ascend', 'descend', 'scythe', 'adolescent' and 'crescent'. Tell them to write the word on one side and draw a picture on the other. Tell them to place their cards picture up in front of a partner and challenge each other to pick a card, guess the word and then spell the word.

Ask the children to complete Unit 19 Resource 2: Scenic spellings. (**Answers** 1. scissors, 2. scent, 3. sciences, 4. fascinating, 5. crescent, 6. descent, 7. muscles, 8. scenic)

Ask the children to write a 100-word description about the ascent and descent of a mountain and the scenic scenery seen from the top, using as many /s/ spelt 'sc' words they can think of. Give them the words from their spelling lists (see Spelling test) if they need inspiration.

Challenge

Ask these children to investigate the meanings of the homophones and near-homophones 'scent' and 'sent', 'decent' and 'descent', 'seen' and 'scene', 'muscles' and 'mussels', 'ascent' and 'assent'. Ask them to create posters illustrating the different meanings of the words.

Homework / Additional activities

Spelling test

Ask the children to learn one of the following lists of words for a spelling test. Challenge them to write sentences for five of the words on their list.

Core words		Support words		Challenge words	
fascinate	muscles	ascent	scene	fascinate	science
scythe	scenic	descent	scenery	fascinating	muscles
ascent	scene	science	scent	adolescent	scenic
ascend	scenery	muscles	scissors	discipline	scene
descend	scent	scenic	crescent	scythe	scenery
descent	scissors			ascent	scent
science	crescent			ascend	scissors
				descend	crescent
				descent	

Collins Connect: Unit 19

Ask the children to complete Unit 19 (see Teach → Year 4 → Spelling → Unit 19).

Unit 20: The /ay/ sound spelt ei, eigh and ey

Overview

English curriculum objectives
- Words with the /ay/ sound spelt ei, eigh, or ey

Treasure House resources
- Spelling Skills Pupil Book 4, Unit 20, pages 46–47
- Collins Connect Treasure House Spelling Year 4, Unit 20

- Photocopiable Unit 20, Resource 1: /ay/ homophones, page 122
- Photocopiable Unit 20, Resource 2: Obey the spelling rules, page 123

Additional resources
- Word cards: sleigh, weigh, weight, eight, eighteen, neighbour, beige, they, grey, obey, prey, reindeer
- Bags to draw word cards from

Introduction

Teaching overview

The long /ay/ sound can be spelt 'ei', as in 'vein', 'rein' and 'veil', 'eigh', as in 'eight', 'weight' and 'neighbour' and 'ey', as in 'grey', 'prey' and 'obey'. Although there are quite a few words with this spelling, many of them are quite specialist words, for example, 'sheikh', 'rein', 'veil', 'sleigh' and 'abseil'.

Introduce the concept

Organise the children into groups and give each table a set of word cards from Unit 20 Resource 1: /ay/ homophones. On your signal, have the groups race against each other to pair the homophones. (**Answers** ate, eight; prey, pray; slay, sleigh; way,

weigh; sheikh, shake; weight, wait; rain, reign; veil, vale; vein, vain; neigh, nay)

Afterwards, write the homophone pairs on the board and discuss the meanings and spelling of each word. Give particular attention to the words 'sheikh' (an Arab leader), 'reign' (rule), 'nay' (no), 'vale' (valley), 'vain' (proud). Sort the words into the different spelling patterns for /ay/: 'ay', 'a–e', 'ai', 'ei', 'eigh' and 'ey'. Introduce other words with the 'ei', 'eigh' or 'ey' spelling pattern, asking the children to suggest words that they know, for example, 'neighbour', 'they', 'obey', 'convey', 'survey', 'reindeer', 'abseil', 'beige' and 'rein'. Add each new word to the relevant group on the board. Again, spend time ensuring the children understand the meanings of these words.

Pupil practice

Pupil Book pages 46–47

Get started

The children rearrange jumbled letters to spell words. Display the correct words (see answers below) to help the children complete the activity. Encourage them to look for the letters to spell the 'ei', 'eigh' or 'ey' clusters first and then see what letters they have left to work out the rest of the word.

Answers
1. *neigh*		[example]
2. convey		[1 mark]
3. neighbour		[1 mark]
4. veil		[1 mark]
5. obey		[1 mark]
6. weigh		[1 mark]
7. grey		[1 mark]
8. eight		[1 mark]

Try these

The children copy and complete sentences by choosing the correct spelling of each missing word. Ensure that the children are familiar enough with these words to be able to recognise the correct spellings. Afterwards, sort the words into the different spelling patterns.

Answers
1. *Tracey chose <u>beige</u> shoes for the party.* [example]

2. The horses in the stable <u>neighed</u>. [1 mark]

3. The well-trained horse always <u>obeyed</u> his master. [1 mark]

4. There are many <u>reindeer</u> in Lapland. [1 mark]

5. When it snows, I play on my <u>sleigh</u>. [1 mark]

6. Jack was learning to <u>abseil</u>. [1 mark]

7. We use birthday cards to <u>convey</u> our greetings. [1 mark]

8. Her face was hidden by her bridal <u>veil</u>. [1 mark]

Now try these

The children compose sentences using the target words 'neighbour', 'beige', 'survey', 'reign', 'veil', 'weigh' and 'weightlifter'. Read the words together and ensure that the children understand the meaning of each. Afterwards, share the children's sentences.

Answers

Beth's <u>neighbour</u> Chris is really good at football. [example]

Accept any sentences where the target word is correctly spelt and used. [7 marks: 1 mark per sentence]

Support, embed & challenge

Support

Ask the children to work in pairs and provide each pair with copies of Unit 20 Resource 1: /ay/ homophones. Help them to pair the homophones. (**Answers** ate, eight; prey, pray; slay, sleigh; way, weigh; sheikh, shake; weight, wait; rain, reign; veil, vale; vein, vain; neigh, nay)

Recap on the meaning of each word. Tell the children to place the words in front of them. Give the children word clues (focussing on the word with this unit's spelling patterns). The children should race to pick up the correct card. Clues could be: 'the sound a horse makes', 'a tube that carries your blood', 'to rule', 'cloth that covers a woman's face', and so on.

Organise the children into pairs. Tell them to use the words cut out from Unit 20 Resource 1 to play a game of 'Pairs'. Explain that they should be looking for pairs of homophones.

Embed

Organise the children into groups and give each group a set of word cards and a bag (see Additional resources). Tell them to read the words and discuss the spelling and meaning of each, spending time trying to memorise the words and their spellings. Ask them to put the cards into the bag. Tell them to take turns to pull a word out of the bag and then do their best to enact the meaning of the word, or to describe the word without using the word being described if it cannot be enacted. The rest of the group must guess the word and write it down. The children can either work as a group to guess and correctly spell the word or work individually, racing each other to guess and spell the word first.

Ask the children to complete Unit 20 Resource 2: Obey the spelling rules. (**Answers** 1. sleigh, 2. weigh, 3. eighteen, 4. neighbour, 5. survey, 6. grey, 7. abseil, 8. prey, 9. veil, 10. obey)

Challenge

Ask these children to find out the difference between an abseil and a zip line. (An abseil goes vertically down; a zip line goes between two points.) Challenge these children to find as many words with the word 'weight' in as they can. (There are many sport-related compound words with 'weight' in them.)

Homework / Additional activities

Spelling test

Ask the children to learn one of the following lists of words for a spelling test. Challenge them to write sentences for five of the words on their list.

Core words		Support words		Challenge words	
sleigh	survey	they	grey	sleigh	convey
weigh	grey	sleigh	obey	weigh	beige
weight	obey	weight	reindeer	weight	rein
eight	prey	eight		eighteen	veil
eighteen	reindeer	eighteen		neighbour	veins
neighbour	abseil	neighbour		survey	reindeer
	veil			grey	sheikh
	veins			obey	abseil
				prey	

Collins Connect: Unit 20

Ask the children to complete Unit 20 (see Teach → Year 4 → Spelling → Unit 20).

# Unit 21: The possessive apostrophe with plural words

Overview

English curriculum objectives

- Possessive apostrophe with plural words

Treasure House resources

- Spelling Skills Pupil Book 4, Unit 21, pages 48–49
- Collins Connect Treasure House Spelling Year 4, Unit 21

- Photocopiable Unit 21, Resource 1: Today's challenge, page 124
- Photocopiable Unit 21, Resource 2: Plural nouns and possessive apostrophes, page 125

Introduction

Teaching overview

Note: to avoid confusion with apostrophes, all letters, phrases and sentences that you will discuss with the children are in italics in this Unit. The correct placing of the possessive apostrophe can catch most people out at times. The rules for adding possessive apostrophes to plural nouns are:

1. If the plural noun ends with an *s*, then just add the apostrophe, for example, *the twins' party*, *the cherries' pips*, *the trees' roots*.

2. If the plural noun does not end with an *s* then add apostrophe + *s*, for example, *the men's cheering*, *the people's princess*.

When trying to decide where to put the apostrophe, children must first establish whether the *s* at the end of a word denotes a plural, a possessive singular or a possessive plural.

Introduce the concept

Write the following sentences on the board and ask the children to help you decide which need an apostrophe: *This weeks spellings are on the board. My slippers are cosy. I have been learning the keyboard for five years. The womans shoes went clickety-clack.* Agree that *week's* and *woman's* need

apostrophes. Illustrate this by turning the sentences around to indicate possession using *of* rather than an apostrophe: *The spellings of this week are on the board. The shoes of the woman went clickety-clack.* Point out that, when the sentences are constructed in this way, there is no *s* after *week* or *woman*. So, we know that the *s* is only there to denote possession and therefore the apostrophe goes before the *s*.

Introduce the rule for adding the apostrophe to plural nouns. Change the first and fourth sentences to *The next two weeks spellings …* and *The womens shoes …* Reconfigure the sentences as before to find out if there is still an *s* at the ends of *week* and *women*: *The spellings of the next two weeks … The shoes of the women …* Explain that there is still an *s* at the end of *weeks*. This means that *weeks* is plural and so the apostrophe goes after the *s* (in the sentence's original configuration). However, there is no *s* at the end of *women* because it is a plural (collective) noun. So, in the sentence's original configuration, the apostrophe goes before the *s*.

Formally recap the rules for adding apostrophes to plurals. Organise the children into groups and ask them to work together to correct the following phrases: *a box of CD's, apple's and orange's, next weeks assembly, both Year 5 classrooms carpets will be replaced.*

Pupil practice

Pupil Book pages 48–49

Get started

The children sort nouns with possessive apostrophes into two groups: singular and plural. Recap with the children on the position of the apostrophe with singular and plural nouns.

Answers

Singular		Plural	
lion's	[1 mark]	*horses'*	*[example]*
class's	[1 mark]	actresses'	[1 mark]
hero's	[1 mark]	children's	[1 mark]

Try these

Read the sentences together and discuss whether the missing word is plural or singular and how they know. Ask the children to choose the appropriate option.

Answers

1. *The <u>policemen's</u> whistles were loud.*   [example]
2. The <u>mouse's</u> cheese was hard.   [1 mark]
3. Both <u>boats'</u> flags were black.   [1 mark]
4. The <u>choir's</u> conductor was ready.   [1 mark]
5. <u>Bess's</u> friends were coming for tea.   [1 mark]

6. The <u>chef's</u> cake mix was in his bowl. [1 mark]

7. One <u>boy's</u> shoes were missing. [1 mark]

8. The <u>children's</u> supper was ready. [1 mark]

Now try these

The children rewrite phases to use a possessive apostrophe instead of the words *that belong to the*. Before they do so, ask them to copy the phrases from the Pupil Book and to work out which words are plural and which possess something.

Afterwards, establish that, in the original phrases, the second noun owns the first noun and that, to get rid

of the words *that belong to the* and use a possessive apostrophe instead, they must put the possessive noun ahead of the noun it owns.

Answers

1. *The lions' manes*	*[example]*
2. The ships' sails	[1 mark]
3. The cricketers' bats	[1 mark]
4. The men's phones	[1 mark]
5. The children's sweets	[1 mark]
6. The farmers' fields	[1 mark]

Support, embed & challenge

Support

Work on sets of singular and plural sentences with these children. Dictate the first sentence then ask the children to work in pairs to decide where the apostrophe goes. When they are happy with their choice, provide the plural version and talk about how this affects the position of the apostrophe.

The girl's bag was on the floor.
The girls' bags were on the floor.

We are going on a week's holiday.
We are going on two weeks' holiday.

The car's wheels skid on the ice.
The cars' wheels skid on the ice.

The man's sneeze was very loud.
The men's sneezes were very loud.

Ask the children to complete Unit 21 Resource 1: Today's challenge. (**Answers** 1. singular, 2. plural, 3. singular, 4. plural, 5. singular; 1. trousers', 2. fishes', 3. tree's, 4. twins', 5. Today's)

Embed

Ask the children to complete Unit 21 Resource 2: Plural nouns and possessive apostrophes. Before they start, explain how the second version of each

sentence helps them. (**Answers** 1. week's, 2. weeks', 3. Niall's, 4. boys', 5. car's, 6. cars', 7. sister's, 8. sisters', 9. snake's, 10. snakes', 11. day's, 12. days', 13. father's, 14. fathers', 15. child's, 16. children's)

Dictate the following sentences to the children for them to write down and decide where the apostrophe should go. When they have written all the sentences, ask them to confer with a partner to check each other's choices. Once they have done so, write the sentences on the board for the children to mark their work and correct any mistakes.

You need a good night's sleep tonight.

I need your parents' permission if you want to do that.

Check your bicycle's tyres and brakes before you set off.

The children's disappointment was clear.

We were at the journey's end at last.

Challenge

Ask these children to spend the week looking, at home, at school and out and about, for phrases that misuse the apostrophe. Tell them to look at market signs, van signs, leaflets through their door and so on. Share any examples that they find with the class and, together, write the phrase with the apostrophe used correctly.

Homework / additional activities

Spelling test

Ask the children to learn the following phrases. Challenge most children to write a sentence for five of the phrases. Challenge more able children to write sentences for the last five phrases.

Penny's hat	the boys' toilets	your heart's desire
the goat's beard	all the cars' engines	this week's spelling
the water's edge	many girls' screams	next month's topic
Amir's house	the drivers' cars	in two months' time
the children's pegs	the year's end	a good night's sleep
the women's laughter		

Collins Connect: Unit 21

Ask the children to complete Unit 21 (see Teach → Year 4 → Spelling → Unit 21).

Unit 22: Homophones and near-homophones (1)

Overview

English curriculum objectives
- Homophones and near-homophones

Treasure House resources
- Spelling Skills Pupil Book 4, Unit 22, pages 50–51
- Collins Connect Treasure House Spelling Year 4, Unit 22
- Photocopiable Unit 22, Resource 1: Whose pairs?, page 126

- Photocopiable Unit 22, Resource 2: Whether to use 'weather' or 'whether', page 127

Additional resources
- Word cards: bury, berry, accept, except, medal, meddle, who's, whose, affect, effect, weather, whether, buries, berries, medals, meddles
- Bags to draw definitions from

Introduction

Teaching overview

This unit covers the following homophones: 'bury' (cover), 'berry' (fruit), 'accept' (consent to), 'except' (excluding), 'medal' (award), 'meddle' (tamper), 'who's' ('who is' or 'who has'), 'whose' (of whom), 'affect' (make a difference to), 'effect' (result or consequence), 'weather' (climate), 'whether' (if). The trickiest of these is the difference between 'affect' and 'effect'. These words will be covered again in Years 5 and 6 so, at this stage, it is worth sticking to the simplest definition: 'affect' is a verb (for example, 'The weather affects my mood.') and 'effect' is a noun (for example, 'We created a nice effect with coloured lights.').

Introduce the concept

Ask the children to work in pairs and hand out a word card to each pair of children (see Additional resources). Ask them to find the pair of children with the word that sounds the same but is spelt differently. When the pairs find each other, ask them to discuss the meanings of the two words in their groups of

four. Ask each group of four to come to the front and write their two words on the board. With the words displayed on the board, read out the meaning of each word (see below). Ask the children to write the word that matches the definition on their whiteboard and hold it up. Tell them to take care to choose the right spelling to match the meaning.

'accept': take something offered; 'except': everything or everyone else but this; 'bury': put in the ground and cover completely; 'berry': small juicy red or purple fruit; 'meddle': interfere; 'medal': a metal disk on a ribbon; 'weather': the conditions outside, for example, rain, snow or sunshine; 'whether': if; 'affect': influence; 'effect': cause; 'who's': who is; 'whose': belonging to whom.

Focus for a moment on 'affect' and 'effect'. Agree that these words are tricky but the most straightforward difference is that 'affect' is a verb. To help them remember this, encourage them to think of this word as 'to affect'. Explain that 'effect' is a noun and they should think of this as 'the/an effect', as in 'the special effects'.

Pupil practice

Pupil Book pages 50–51

Get started

The children match words to their meanings. Read the words together and clarify the meaning of each.

Answers

1. *except*   *[example]*
2. whether   [1 mark]
3. affect   [1 mark]
4. berry   [1 mark]
5. accept   [1 mark]
6. meddle   [1 mark]
7. bury   [1 mark]
8. medal   [1 mark]

Try these

The children copy and complete sentences by choosing the correct homophones to fill the gaps. Ask the children to read each sentence and decide which spelling matches the meaning they need to complete it.

Answers

1. *Serena walked to the front of the hall to* *accept her prize.*   *[example]*
2. The bird ate the <u>berries</u> from the bush.   [1 mark]

3. The <u>weather</u> had started to clear up, so Kamal decided to go out. [1 mark]

4. Mrs Jones, <u>whose</u> cat was lost, always hoped he'd return. [1 mark]

5. Samantha's sister told her not to <u>meddle</u> with her jewellery. [1 mark]

6. The recent bad weather <u>affected</u> the harvest. [1 mark]

7. The athlete was awarded a gold <u>medal</u>. [1 mark]

8. The film had excellent special <u>effects</u>. [1 mark]

Now try these

The children compose sentences using the target words 'except', 'accept', 'bury', 'medal', 'effect', 'weather', 'who's' and 'meddle'. Suggest that the children discuss sentence ideas with a partner before writing them down.

Answers

Taylor disliked all sports <u>except</u> football. [example]

Accept any sentences where the target word is correctly spelt and used. [8 marks: 1 mark per sentence]

Support, embed & challenge

Support

Provide each child with a copy of Unit 22 Resource 1: <u>Whose</u> pairs?, and instruct them to cut out the words. Ask them to sort the words into homophone pairs. Discuss the meaning of each word. Ask them to cut out the definitions from Unit 22 Resource 1 and match each one to the correct word. Put a set of the definitions in a bag. Ask the children to take turns to pull a definition from the bag and to read it out to the group. Everyone else in the group must select and hold up the corresponding word. Organise the children into pairs and ask them to play a game of 'Pairs' using the words and definitions from Unit 22 Resource 1 where a pair is a word and its definition. (**Answers** bury – cover completely, berry – small fruit; medal – metal disk, meddle – interfere; except – not including, accept – consent to; whose – of whom, who's – who is; effect – result, affect – influence; weather – climate, whether – if)

Embed

Ask the children to complete Unit 22 Resource 2: <u>Whether</u> to use '<u>weather</u>' or '<u>whether</u>'.

(**Answers** 1. medal, 2. accept, 3. berries, 4. except, 5. whose, 6. whether, 7. affect, 8. effect, 9. who's, 10. meddle)

Spend time practising the difference between 'affect' and 'effect' by asking the children to complete the following sentences.

'The poor sound quality _____ our enjoyment of the film.'

'We created a nice snow _____ with lights and ticker tape.'

'The film had awesome special _____.'

'Climate change _____ us all.'

Ask the children to compose two sentences of their own: one using 'affect' and one using 'effect'.

Challenge

Ask these children to investigate the meanings of the English phrases 'bury your feelings' and 'bury your light under a bushel'.

Homework / additional activities

Spelling test

Ask the children to learn the following sentences.

The pirates found the buried treasure.	The weather was not warm enough for a picnic.
I got red berry juice on my white T-shirt.	Tina doesn't know whether she can come today.
Please accept my apology.	Too many late nights affected my school work.
Everyone in my family has had chicken pox except me.	Your stomach ache is the effect of too many sweets!
Whose birthday is it today?	Gemma's been meddling with the stuff in my room!
Guess who's coming to dinner.	Everyone who finished the race was given a medal.

Collins Connect: Unit 22

Ask the children to complete Unit 22 (see Teach → Year 4 → Spelling → Unit 22).

Unit 23: Homophones and near-homophones (2)

Overview

English curriculum objectives
- Homophones and near-homophones

Treasure House resources
- Spelling Skills Pupil Book 4, Unit 23, pages 52–53
- Collins Connect Treasure House Spelling Year 4, Unit 23

- Photocopiable Unit 23, Resource 1: Throw <u>here</u>, <u>not</u> there!, page 128
- Photocopiable Unit 23, Resource 2: <u>Great</u> spelling practise!, page 129

Additional resources
- Counters (for Resource 1)
- Bags to draw words and definitions from

Introduction

Teaching overview

This unit covers the homophones 'hear' (detect sound), 'here' (this place), 'grate' (shred with a grater), 'great' (big or wonderful), 'not' (used to form a negative), 'knot' (fastening of looped rope or string), 'grown' (past participle of 'grow'), 'groan' (inarticulate sound conveying pleasure or pain), 'heel' (back part of the foot), 'heal' (become healthy again) and 'he'll' (contraction of 'he will'). Most of these words are pretty straightforward, although some of the meanings of 'grate' might not be known to all children: 'to shred with a grater', 'to scrape', 'to annoy' and 'a frame for a fire'.

Introduce the concept

Write the words 'hear', 'here', 'grate', 'great', 'not', 'knot', 'grown', 'groan', 'heel', 'heal' and 'he'll' on the board. Organise the children into groups. Ask each group to choose a word, to say the word and to tell you what the word means or to use it in a sentence. Award a mark for each correct definition/sentence. Cross the words off when they are chosen. This activity will get harder as it progresses and the last groups have a choice of only the most difficult words. When the children get stuck, explain the meanings of the remaining words. Challenge the children to provide more definitions for 'grate'.

Pupil practice

Pupil Book pages 52–53

Get started

The children match words to their meanings. Tell the children to check the meaning of each word before choosing the correct spelling to match the meaning.

Answers

1. *grown*	*[example]*
2. he'll	[1 mark]
3. grate	[1 mark]
4. groan	[1 mark]
5. here	[1 mark]
6. knot	[1 mark]
7. heal	[1 mark]
8. great	[1 mark]

Try these

The children copy and complete sentences by choosing the correct homophones to the fill the gaps. Tell the children to read the sentences carefully and to use the contexts of the sentences to choose the correct spellings.

Answers

1. *Charlie's grandmother said, "You've <u>grown</u>!"*

[example]

2. "There are spaces over <u>here</u>," said Julie. [1 mark]

3. If he puts his coat on <u>he'll</u> feel much warmer. [1 mark]

4. Marek wished he had <u>not</u> eaten all the sweets. [1 mark]

5. Everyone thought the disco was <u>great</u>. [1 mark]

6. The new trainers caused blisters on her <u>heel</u>. [1 mark]

7. At dawn you can <u>hear</u> the birds start to sing. [1 mark]

8. I like to <u>grate</u> cheese on top of my spaghetti. [1 mark]

Now try these

The children write sentences to use the target words 'not', 'groan', 'hear', 'knot', 'grate', 'he'll', 'heal' and 'grown'. Suggest that the children discuss sentence ideas with a partner before writing them down.

Answers

Janet wished she had <u>not</u> left her hat unguarded.   *[example]*

Accept any sentences where the target word is correctly spelt and used. [8 marks: 1 mark per sentence]

Support, embed & challenge

Support

Organise the children into pairs and give each pair a counter and a copy of Unit 23 Resource 1: Throw <u>here</u>, <u>not</u> there! Ask them to take turns to throw the counter and say the definition or spell the word, continuing until they have both landed on each square. (**Answers** here – this place, great – wonderful, groan – moan, not – forms a negative, hear – detect sound, grate – shred, grown – became bigger, heel – back of a foot, knot – tangle, heal – recover)

Tell the children to cut out the words and definitions from Unit 23 Resource 1 and put them in a bag. Still working in their pairs, the children should take turns to draw from the bag. If the child selects a definition, they must say the word it defines and then spell it. If the child selects a word, they must use the word in a sentence.

Embed

Ask the children to complete Unit 23 Resource 2: <u>Great</u> spelling practise! (**Answers** 1. he'll, 2. hear, 3. groan, 4. here, 5. not, 6. grate, 7. great, 8. grown, 9. heals, 10. heels, 11. knot)

Ask the children to learn the following sentences for the word 'grate': 'That loud music is really grating my nerves!' 'It really grates on me when I see the apostrophe used wrongly.' 'Cleaning out the grate after a fire is a dirty job.'

Ask the children to write their own sentences for the homophones covered in this unit. They should write one sentence per homophone pair. For example: 'Come here and see if you can hear it too.' 'The blister on my heel is slowly healing.' 'It's not difficult to tie a reef knot.' 'Mum groans when she hears I've grown out of my shoes.' 'It would be great if you could grate the cheese for me.'

Challenge

Challenge these children to use all ten words in a single paragraph. Provide these children with more pairs of homophones to learn: 'scent' and 'sent', 'fined' and 'find', 'chilly' and 'chilli', 'horse' and 'hoarse', 'key' and 'quay', 'flee' and 'flea', 'leek' and 'leak', 'flew' and 'flu', 'alter' and 'altar', 'cereal' and 'serial'.

Homework / Additional activities

Spelling test

Ask the children to learn the following sentences.

I can hear the sea.
Hoorah, they're here!
Grated carrot is nicer than boiled carrot.
My great-grandmother is pretty great!
This cream will help your cut heal.
He'll be here any minute.
My stomach was in a knot before my exam.
No, it's not here!
The sunflowers we planted have grown tall.
"Oh, no! It's raining!" we groan.

Collins Connect: Unit 23

Ask the children to complete Unit 23 (see Teach → Year 4 → Spelling → Unit 23).

Unit 24: Homophones and near-homophones (3)

Overview

English curriculum objectives

- Homophones and near-homophones

Treasure House resources

- Spelling Skills Pupil Book 4, Unit 24, pages 54–55
- Collins Connect Treasure House Spelling Year 4, Unit 24
- Photocopiable Unit 23, Resource 1: Throw <u>here</u>, <u>not</u> there!, page 128
- Photocopiable Unit 24, Resource 1: Play <u>fair</u>, page 130

- Photocopiable Unit 24, Resource 2: Have you missed these homophones? page 131

Additional resources

- Word cards: mist, missed, mane, main, plane, plain, peace, piece, meet, meat, fair, fare, here, hear, groan, grown, grate, great, not, knot, heel, heal, bury, berry, accept, except, medal, meddle, who's, whose, affect, effect
- Counters (for Resource 1)
- Bags to draw words and definitions from

Introduction

Teaching overview

This unit covers the homophones 'mist' (light fog), 'missed' (failed to hit), 'mane' (long hair on the head or neck of a mammal), 'main' (chief or foremost), 'plane' (aircraft), 'plain' (undecorated or obvious), 'peace' (calm or quiet), 'piece' (bit of something), 'meet' (come into the presence of), 'meat' (flesh as food), 'fair' (equal or just) and 'fare' (cost of a ticket to travel).

Introduce the concept

Organise the children into teams. Provide each team with a set of word cards (see Additional resources).

On your signal, the teams should race to sort the words into their homophone pairs. Emphasise working together as a team, reminding the children that working well together will get the job done faster. The first team to sort all their cards wins. Ask each member of the winning team to choose a homophone to say out loud. The other teams must spell the two words that are pronounced like that. Ask the children to identify the new homophone pairs for this unit. Write this unit's words on the board and ask the children to help you write a definition for each one.

Pupil practice

Pupil Book pages 54–55

Get started

The children match words to their meanings. Before they do so, ask them to find any words in the box that are homophones pairs (meat – meet, fair – fare). Tell them to turn to a partner and discuss the meaning of each word in the box.

Answers

1. *plane*	*[example]*
2. meet	[1 mark]
3. mist	[1 mark]
4. peace	[1 mark]
5. mane	[1 mark]
6. meat	[1 mark]
7. fair	[1 mark]
8. fare	[1 mark]

Try these

The children copy and complete sentences by choosing the correct homophones to fill the gaps. Tell the children to read the sentences carefully and to use the contexts of the sentences to choose the correct spellings.

Answers

1. *The weather forecast was for <u>mist</u> on the hills.*	*[example]*
2. Jake <u>missed</u> his friend now that he was gone.	[1 mark]
3. Lucas liked his biscuits <u>plain</u>, without chocolate.	[1 mark]
4. "Would you like a <u>piece</u> of cake?" asked Peyton.	[1 mark]
5. The <u>main</u> meal was to be eaten at 1 p.m.	[1 mark]
6. I plan to <u>meet</u> my friend at 3 p.m, today.	[1 mark]

7. "How much is the bus <u>fare</u> to town?"   [1 mark]

8. As the last children left, there was <u>peace</u> again.

                                                  [1 mark]

Now try these

The children compose sentences using the target words 'mane', 'mist', 'plane', 'peace', 'meat', 'fair', 'fare' and 'plain'. Tell the children to share their sentence ideas with a partner.

Answers

The lion's <u>mane</u> was long and thick.   *[example]*

Accept any sentences where the target word is correctly spelt and used. [8 marks: 1 mark per sentence]

Support, embed & challenge

Support

Organise the children into pairs and give each pair a counter and a copy of Unit 24 Resource 1: Play <u>fair</u>. Ask them to take turns to throw the counter and say the definition or spell the word, continuing until they have both ticked each square. (**Answers** meet – encounter, plane – aircraft, fair – light or pleasant, mane – long hair, piece – part of something, fare – cost of travel, meat – animal flesh, plain – obvious or basic, missed – failed to catch, peace – calmness, main – most important, mist – light fog)

Cut out the words and definitions from Unit 24 Resource 1 and reuse the words and definitions from Unit 23 Resource 1: Throw <u>here</u>, <u>not</u> there! Put them all in a bag. Take turns in the group to draw from the bag and either spell the word (if the child picks a definition) or use the word in a sentence (if the child picks a word). Use both sets of words to play a game of 'Pairs', first matching homophones (without using the definitions) then with all the cards, pairing words and definitions.

Embed

Ask the children to work in pairs and provide each pair with Unit 24 Resource 1: Play <u>fair</u> and Unit 23

Resource 1: Throw <u>here</u>, <u>not</u> there! Ask them to cut out the words and definitions and to use them to play a game of 'Pairs', matching words to their definitions. Afterwards, provide each pair with a bag and tell them to put the words in it. Tell them to take turns with their partner to draw two words from the bag and to make up a sentence using them. Next, tell the children to put the definitions into the bag and to take turns to draw a definition from the bag, read it to their partner and then spell the word. They can keep the definition if they spell the word correctly.

Ask the children to complete Unit 24 Resource 2: Have you missed these homophones? (**Answers** 1. plain, 2. plane, 3. main, 4. meet, 5. mist, 6. mane, 7. fare, 8. missed, 9. fair, 10. piece)

Challenge

Challenge these children to learn the meanings and spelling of these homophones:

'coarse' and 'course', 'flour' and 'flower', 'need' and 'knead', 'aloud' and 'allowed', 'tail' and 'tale', 'roll' and 'role', 'board' and 'bored', 'hole' and 'whole', 'waste' and 'waist', 'you' and 'ewe'.

Homework / additional activities

Spelling test

Ask the children to learn the following sentences.

The mist in the valley made islands of the hills.	Can I have five minutes' peace to drink my tea?
Auntie Caroline missed my birthday.	I have a new piece to learn on the keyboard.
The male peacock has a huge display of feathers.	I'll meet you outside school at 3 p.m.
The main problem is the rain.	A vegetarian does not eat meat.
The plane took off with a roar.	"It's not fair!" cried Claire.
Take a piece of plain paper for your pictures.	The girls paid the bus fare and raced upstairs.

Collins Connect: Unit 24

Ask the children to complete Unit 24 (see Teach → Year 4 → Spelling → Unit 24).

Unit 25: Homophones and near-homophones (4)

Overview

English curriculum objectives
- Homophones and near-homophones

Treasure House resources
- Spelling Skills Pupil Book 4, Unit 25, pages 56–57
- Collins Connect Treasure House Spelling Year 4, Unit 25
- Photocopiable Unit 25, Resource 1: Win the game: reign supreme!, page 132

- Photocopiable Unit 25, Resource 2: Homophones to make you bawl, page 133

Additional resources
- Word cards: ball, bawl, male, mail, brake, break, rain, rein, reign, seen, scene
- Word cards from Unit 24
- Counters to complete Resource 1
- Bags to draw word cards from

Introduction

Teaching overview

This unit covers the homophones 'ball' (sphere), 'bawl' (cry loudly), 'male' (gender), 'mail' (post), 'brake' (mechanically slow a vehicle), 'break' (come apart), 'rain' (precipitation), 'rein' (guide straps), 'reign' (rule), 'seen' (past participle of 'see') and 'scene' (location or section of a play). The word 'mail' is used less commonly in the UK than 'post' or 'email' but should still be familiar to the children.

Introduce the concept

Give each child a word card (see Additional resources), taking a card yourself if you have an odd number of children. Choose the homophones you want to practise, as you will have more words than children. Provide more able children with the

trickier words. Tell the children to search the room to find their homophone (or near-homophone) partner. Inform them that there will be two trios: 'he'll', 'heel', 'heal' and 'rain', 'rein', 'reign'. Tell them to discuss the meanings of the two/three words with their partner/s, then hide them behind their backs and practise spelling them. Tell them to ask for help if they need their word meanings clarifying. Ask the children with this unit's target words to come to the front in pairs and introduce their words. Point out the recent spelling patterns 'ei' for /ay/ and 'sc' for /s/. Ask the children with word cards for 'bawl' and 'ball' to stand up and discuss what they think 'bawl' means. Encourage them to remember the work they did on these homophones in Year 3. Clarify the meanings of 'rein' and 'reign'.

Pupil practice

Pupil Book pages 56–57

Get started

The children match words to their meanings. Before they do so, ask the children to find the three homophones pairs. Tell them to turn to a partner and discuss the meaning of each word.

Answers

1. *brake*	*[example]*
2. bawl	[1 mark]
3. male	[1 mark]
4. seen	[1 mark]
5. reign	[1 mark]
6. rain	[1 mark]
7. ball	[1 mark]
8. scene	[1 mark]

Try these

The children copy and complete sentences by choosing the correct homophones to fill the gaps. Tell the children to read the sentences carefully and to use the contexts of the sentences to choose the correct spellings.

Answers

1. *The burglar had to <u>break</u> the window to get in.* *[example]*

2. The tennis <u>ball</u> crossed the line. [1 mark]

3. The old man <u>reined</u> in his mule. [1 mark]

4. The postman delivered my <u>mail</u> on time this morning. [1 mark]

5. The <u>scene</u> needed more rehearsal. [1 mark]

6. Queen Elizabeth II has <u>reigned</u> for over 60 years. [1 mark]

7. <u>Rain</u> has fallen in the valleys today.   [1 mark]

8. I have <u>seen</u> lightning in the sky tonight.   [1 mark]

Now try these

The children compose sentences using the target words 'seen', 'brake', 'bawl', 'male', 'rein', 'scene', 'mail' and 'break'. Suggest that the children discuss sentence ideas with a partner before writing them down.

Answers

Sabir had <u>seen</u> the whole match.   *[example]*

Accept any sentences where the target word is correctly spelt and used. [8 marks: 1 mark per sentence]

Support, embed & challenge

Support

Work with these children on recognising the meanings of as many words as possible. Ask the children to complete Unit 25 Resource 1: Win the game: <u>reign</u> supreme! (**Answers** rain – water from the sky, break – fall apart or stop working, bawl – cry or shout, seen – past of 'see', scene – site or location, mail – post, reign – rule, brake – stop mechanically, male – not female, rein – straps to control horses)

Ask the children to cut out the words and definitions from Unit 25 Resource 1 and use them to play a game of 'Pairs', matching words and definitions.

Put all the word cards (see Additional resources) in a bag and ask the children to take turns to draw a card from the bag, read it out and put it in the centre of the group. The next child takes a card out and places the card down next to the first. Carry on until someone spots a pair of homophones. They should shout 'Snap!' and can keep the pair if they can give a definition for each word. The children should continue until all the words have been paired up.

Embed

Organise the children into groups of three and provide each group with word cards (see Additional resources) in a bag. First, ask the children to play a game of 'Snap': they take turns to draw a card from the bag, read it out and put it in the centre of the group. When someone spots a pair of homophones, they shout 'Snap!' and can keep the pair if they can give a definition for each word.

Next, ask them to take turns to draw two words from the bag and make up a silly sentence using the two words. The other two children in the group check that the words have been used properly (if not sensibly).

Ask the children to complete Unit 25 Resource 2: Homophones to make you <u>bawl</u>. (**Answers** 1. seen, 2. brake, 3. break, 4. male, 5. scene, 6. rain, 7. ball, 8. rein, 9. bawled)

Challenge

Ask these children to learn the meanings of these homophone (or near-homophone) pairs: 'peak' and 'peek', 'paws' and 'pause', 'sore' and 'saw', 'cell' and 'sell', 'hall' and 'haul', 'already' and 'all ready', 'days' and 'daze', 'round' and 'around', 'none' and 'nun', 'poor', 'pour' and 'pore'.

Homework / additional activities

Spelling test

Ask the children to learn the following sentences.

Please don't kick the ball in the hall.	Would you like to reign for eighty years?
The baby crawled into the corner and bawled.	Have you seen the green tree?
Jake saw the rake and braked quickly.	Max left the room for the scary scene.
We each had a peach at break time.	The computer failed to send my mail.
We listened to the rain gurgle down the drain.	A male duck is called a drake.
Uncle Joe held the horse's reins as we sat on the cart.	

Collins Connect: Unit 25

Ask the children to complete Unit 25 (see Teach → Year 4 → Spelling → Unit 25).

Review unit 3

A. Ask the children to correct the spellings of the misspelt words.

1. vague		[1 mark]
2. unique		[1 mark]
3. plague		[1 mark]
4. scissors		[1 mark]
5. scene		[1 mark]
6. grey		[1 mark]
7. reindeer		[1 mark]
8. muscles		[1 mark]

B. Ask the children to write out the phrases and add the missing apostrophes.

1. the cat's ginger coat	[1 mark]
2. five minutes' peace	[1 mark]
3. the ladies' bags	[1 mark]
4. the horse's mane	[1 mark]
5. two days' extension	[1 mark]
6. James's parents	[1 mark]
7. the bunnies' ears	[1 mark]
8. this term's goals	[1 mark]

C. Ask the children to copy and complete the sentences by choosing the correct words to fill the gaps.

1. I will not <u>accept</u> this piece of work. Do it again!	[1 mark]
2. I'm afraid your poor spelling will <u>affect</u> your mark.	[1 mark]
3. The wires for the headphones have got into a terrible <u>knot</u>.	[1 mark]
4. Can you pass me the cheese <u>grater</u>, please?	[1 mark]
5. We waited at the corner but we must have <u>missed</u> you.	[1 mark]
6. The <u>main</u> reason I've called you here is to ask a favour.	[1 mark]
7. It <u>breaks</u> my heart to see you crying like this.	[1 mark]
8. By the time the police arrived at the <u>scene</u>, the pickpocket had vanished.	[1 mark]

To double or not to double

Sort these words into words where the consonant before the suffix has been doubled and those where it has not.

Underline the strongest stress in each word. Can you see a pattern?

beginner visiting upsetting cancelling opener listener
forbidden limiting offering travelled

Consonant doubled

enrolled

_____
_____
_____
_____

Consonant not doubled

targeted

_____
_____
_____
_____

Removed the suffix from these words and write the root word.
Remember, you might need to take away a consonant.
Underline the syllable in the root word with the strongest stress.

watering _____

forgotten _____

listened _____

enrolling _____

opened _____

admitting _____

offered _____

preferred _____

committed _____

occurred _____

Perfecting your spelling

Circle the correct spelling of each word.

> Remember:
> Stress on the second syllable or ends **l** → double the last letter
> Stress on the first syllable or ends **w** → just add the suffix

preferring	prefering	openner	opener
waterred	watered	occurring	occuring
regretting	regreting	offerring	offering
listenner	listener	travelled	traveled
labelled	labeled	upsetting	upseting
enrolled	enroled	targetting	targeting
visitting	visiting	cancelling	canceling
committing	commiting	limitting	limiting
elbowwed	elbowed	beginner	beginer
admitted	admited	narrowwed	narrowed

Mysterious word search

Find these words in the word search.

gym   myths   syrup   Egypt   symbol   system   crystal   pyramid

bicycle   mystery

a	c	g	g	k	s	y	r	u	p
e	E	g	y	p	t	f	h	d	b
k	p	h	m	h	d	m	k	f	i
m	y	s	t	e	r	y	a	q	c
f	r	y	e	c	q	t	t	x	y
d	a	m	b	j	x	h	z	h	c
q	m	b	c	r	y	s	t	a	l
b	i	o	c	e	j	f	a	d	e
f	d	l	s	y	s	t	e	m	g

Crystal clear spellings

Look at the words at the bottom of the page then fold them under.

Fill in the missing words. All the missing words have the /i/ sound spelt **y**.

1. We went swimming whilst Mum went to the g__ __.

2. Dad read me the Greek m__ __ __ about the minotaur.

3. Would you like s__ __ __ __ on your pancakes?

4. The great Pharaohs were buried inside p__ __ __ __ __ __ __.

5. The c__ __ __ __ __ __ __ sparkled in the light.

6. The Pharaohs ruled E__ __ __ __ for thousands of years.

7. The boys rode their b__ __ __ __ __ __ __ in the park.

8. It is a m__ __ __ __ __ __ where your shoes have gone.

- -

Egypt   syrup   myth   gym   crystals   bicycles   mystery   pyramids

Eleanor and the dragon

Underline the words in the story that have the /u/ sound spelt **ou**. Watch out for words with the /ou/ or /oo/ sounds spelt **ou**!

Write the words at the bottom of the page.

Eleanor wanted to go with her cousins to fight the dragon.

"You're too young," said her mother.

"I won't be any trouble," Eleanor pleaded. "I'm old enough! And brave enough! And tough enough!"

It was true and, in time, her mother agreed.

The road to the dragon's country was rough and the weather was foul. Up hills and down rocks they trudged. Eleanor's cousins soon felt crushed and downhearted but Eleanor told jokes and sang songs to encourage them and made hearty soups to nourish them.

After a couple of days, they arrived at the dragon's cave. Smoke billowed out and Eleanor's cousins' courage failed them. But Eleanor stepped forward and swung her sword with a flourish.

"Come out, Dragon!" she shouted.

The smoke cleared and there stood the mighty dragon: gold scales, red eyes, fiery breath … and about the size of a rabbit!

_____   _____   _____   _____

_____   _____   _____

_____   _____   _____

_____   _____

A r<u>ou</u>gh, t<u>ou</u>gh spelling game

Play this game with a partner. You will need a counter.

Cut out the strips at the bottom of the page and take one each.

Take turns to throw the counter onto a word. Close your eyes and spell the word. If you spell it correctly, you can cross it off your slip.

The winner is the first person to cross off all their words.

Note: you only get one chance per go to throw the counter. If you don't land on a new word, you must wait until your next go.

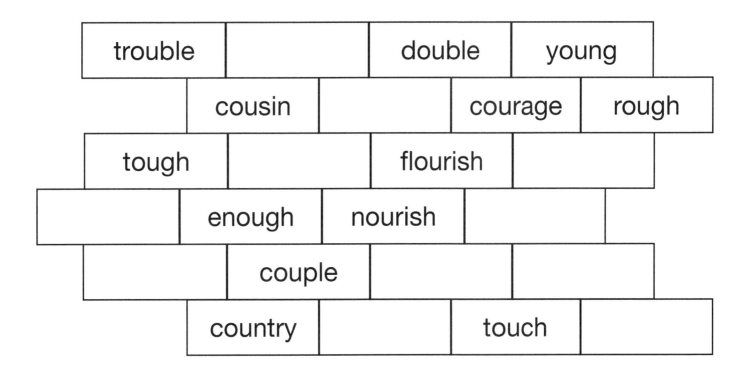

trouble		double	young
cousin		courage	rough
tough		flourish	
	enough	nourish	
	couple		
country		touch	

---

trouble   double   couple   young   cousin   touch   courage
rough   tough   enough   flourish   nourish   country

---

trouble   double   couple   young   cousin   touch   courage
rough   tough   enough   flourish   nourish   country

Are they <u>dis</u>takes or <u>mis</u>takes?

Which of these words exist? Cross out the words that don't.

distaken	mistaken
dislike	mislike
disunderstand	misunderstand
dishonest	mishonest
disappear	misappear
distake	mistake
disabled	misabled
disfortune	misfortune
discomfort	miscomfort
dishap	mishap
disobey	misobey
disrupt	misrupt

Choosing <u>dis</u>– or <u>mis</u>–

Add **dis–** or **mis–** to the words in the box to create a word for each meaning. You will need to use three of the words twice.

honest   leading   count   placed   fortune   continue   used

1. a lower price _____

2. to count wrongly _____

3. no longer being used _____

4. treated badly _____

5. moved from its place _____

6. lost _____

7. bad luck _____

8. stop doing _____

9. not truthful _____

10. gives you the wrong idea _____

Incorrect or imcorrect: which is correct?

Add **in–**, **im–**, **ir–** or **il–** to these words.

Remember the rules.
im–: root words beginning **m** and **p**
il–: root words beginning l
ir–: root words beginning r
in–: all other root words

possible _____   proper _____

relevant _____   exact _____

correct _____   prison _____

legal _____   credible _____

mature _____   patient _____

active _____   responsible _____

Remove the prefix from these words. Write the root word.

incompetent _____

immortal _____

irregular _____

illegible _____

An <u>in</u>complete crossword to complete

Can you solve this crossword? All the answers begin **in–**, **im–**, **il–** or **ir–**.

Across

1. Not patient

3. To put in jail

6. Not possible

7. Not allowed by law

Down

2. Unbelievable or amazing

3. Will live forever

4. Acts younger than their age

5. Too unclear to read

<u>Inter</u>connected meanings

Draw a line to match each word to its meaning.

react	speak when someone else is talking
interrupt	construct or build again
intervene	take away or get rid of
rewrite	network linking computers worldwide
remove	become visible again
international	give an opinion on how good a thing is
rename	put back together
reappear	take action to improve a bad situation
intercity	attempt to deliver again
review	route from one city to another
redeliver	meddle with something
interfere	give something a new name
reassemble	change what was written before
rebuild	of or involving more than one nation
internet	respond to something

Prefix mix

Cut out the words and prefixes. Use the words and prefixes to create as many words as you can. Write down the words you create. Most words will go with at least two different prefixes, such as **in**take, **mis**take and **re**take.

in	re	dis	mis
place	shape	match	cover
action	connect	assemble	fit
locate	name	organised	take
appear	active	plant	ability

Super spellings

Read the two words in each pair. Choose the words that you think exist in English. Cross out the wrong words.

supermarine	submarine
superhero	subhero
superheading	subheading
superstar	substar
superway	subway
superscribe	subscribe
superheated	subheated
supermerge	submerge
superset	subset
superdivide	subdivide
superstore	substore
superpower	subpower
supertract	subtract

Don't <u>sub</u>scribe to <u>sub</u>standard spelling!

Add **super–** or **sub–** to the words in the box and use the new words to complete the sentences.

star	marine	section	merged	glue	market	divided	car

1. We _____ the bicycle tyre in the water to find the puncture.

2. Dad used _____ to stick his glasses back together.

3. The boys _____ the rest of the cake between themselves.

4. Everyone stared as the _____ zoomed down the road.

5. Mum said I was a _____ for tidying the sitting room.

6. Our homework was to read the _____ on frogs.

7. Underwater, the _____ secretly followed the warship.

8. Mum dragged us to the _____ after school to buy vegetables.

Automatically spell correctly

Draw a line to match each word to its meaning.

automatic	opposite to the direction clock hands travel
anticlockwise	liquid that stops things freezing
autobiography	medicine that treats poison
antisocial	stops or prevents infection
antifreeze	behaviour that is bad for others
antidote	story of your own life
autopilot	signature of someone important
antiseptic	moves or activates on its own
automobile	do something without thinking
autograph	an old-fashioned word for a car

Auto– or anti–?

Add **auto–** or **anti–** to these words. Use the new words to complete the sentences.

graph climax freeze pilot social biography
septic clockwise

1. The ending of the film was a real _____.

2. Most things unscrew in an _____ direction.

3. I helped Mum add _____ to the car's engine.

4. My reading book is the _____ of Michael Rosen.

5. Felix waited outside the theatre for the star's _____.

6. I was on _____ and put on my school uniform even though it was Saturday.

7. It is _____ to play loud music when others are trying to sleep.

8. Mrs Peters used an _____ wipe to clean the graze on my knee.

An –<u>ation</u> examin<u>ation</u>

Turn these verbs into nouns by adding –**ation** to the end of each verb. Write the new words. Remember, if the verb ends in **e** you will need to remove the **e** first.

1. inform — *information*

2. tempt — _____

3. inspire — _____

4. prepare — _____

5. examine — _____

6. observe — _____

7. organise — _____

8. explore — _____

Turn these nouns into verbs. Take off the –**ation** suffix. Remember, you might need to add an **e**.

1. reservation — _____

2. expectation — _____

3. recommendation — _____

4. declaration — _____

Experiment<u>ation</u> in adding –<u>ation</u>

Complete this chart by writing the corresponding verb or noun.

Noun	Verb
	invite
transformation	
	install
inspiration	
	destine
confirmation	
	document
starvation	
	experiment
deprivation	
	adapt
realisation	
	civilise
transportation	
	incline
modernisation	
	note
	organise

Adverb pairs

Pair the adverbs with their root words. Write each pair in the correct column of the table.

steady   painful   steadily   painfully

childish   horrible   horribly   healthily

entire   sensible   entirely   sensibly

healthy   terrible   terribly   basically

close   terrific   closely   terrifically

basic   frantic   frantically

grumpy   childishly   grumpily

Just add –ly	Remove **le** then add **–ly**	Turn **y** into **i** then add **–ly**	Add **–ally**

Skilfully and capably spelling words ending –ly

Add –ly to the words in the brackets. Use the new words to complete the sentences.

1. _____ , we're in a pickle.
    (basic)

2. This is _____ your fault!
    (entire)

3. The dance show went _____ well.
    (terrific)

4. The baby's first steps were a bit _____.
    (wobble)

5. This jumper is too _____ and I can't wear it.
    (prickle)

6. The gymnast flipped _____ along the bar.
    (acrobatic)

7. Mum watched _____ from the front row.
    (enthusiastic)

8. Yes, you can have one if you ask _____.
    (polite)

9. Hope hobbled home _____ on her sore foot.
    (painful)

10. The girls got changed _____ for swimming.
    (quick)

Letter match

Use these cards to play a game of 'Letter match'.

You will need four players, a bag, four pens and a willing extra person.

Cut out the letters at the bottom of the page and place them in the bag. Cut out the words and give each player two words (one from each row) and a pen. Ask the willing person to take the letters out of the bag one at a time and to read them out. The players mark off those letters on their words. The first player to cross off all their letters in both words calls out 'Letter match!'

c o m p o s u r e	d i s c l o s u r e	e n c l o s u r e	e x p o s u r e
l e i s u r e	m e a s u r e	p l e a s u r e	t r e a s u r e

a	c	d	e	i	l	m	n	o	p	r	s	t	u	x

It's a plea<u>sure</u> spelling <u>sure</u>

Complete the missing words. Listen to the **/zhur/** or **/sher/** ending to decide on the spelling. The missing words are all ones you've been practising.

1. We went to the l__ __ __ __ __ __ centre to go swimming.

2. It's a p__ __ __ __ __ __ __ __ to meet you.

3. My ears popped from the air pr__ __ __ __ __ __ as we took off.

4. The day felt much f__ __ __ __ __ __ after the storm.

5. The pirates opened the t__ __ __ __ __ __ __ chest and found ... a dead spider.

6. The lion paced angrily inside his en__ __ __ __ __ __ __ .

7. Bam! The can cr__ __ __ __ __ flattened the can.

8. Jacob was very upset when he heard about the cl__ __ __ __ __ of the pizza place.

Nurture your knowledge of –ture

Fill in the missing word in each sentence
(which all end with the /cher/ sound).

1. Mani spooned the cake m__ __ __ __ __ __ into the cake tin.

2. We sat in the d__ __ __ __ __ __ __ __ lounge and waited for our plane.

3. When Harry's gerbil escaped, we all helped to rec__ __ __ __ __ __ it.

4. My little sister is a wild c__ __ __ __ __ __ __ with mad hair and missing teeth.

5. Next week, our class is going on a n__ __ __ __ __ walk to collect leaves and find bugs.

6. Granny has a p__ __ __ __ __ __ of each of her ten grandchildren.

7. When my parents were young, they went on an a__ __ __ __ __ __ __ __ to Australia.

8. In the f__ __ __ __ __ , cars will drive themselves.

A crossword adventure

Can you solve this crossword? All the answers end **–ture**.

Across

2. The measure of heat

4. A large bird that eats dead meat

5. A very small version of something

6. A hole in a car or bicycle wheel

9. A painting in a frame

10. A hand movement or small act with meaning

Down

1. Acts younger than their real age

3. An interesting journey where exciting things happen

7. To take hold of a person you are chasing – or a castle you are invading

8. Your name hand-written on a legal document

Rainforest excur<u>sion</u>

Find the words in this story that have the buzzy /zh/
sound as in trea**sure** or explo**sion**.

Antonio and his mother had just moved from England to
Brazil. Antonio's mother said it would be an adventure.
Antonio was not so happy about it. However, his
mother's new job was researching soil erosion in the
Amazon rainforest and that meant she needed to live
here.

   This weekend, to cheer Antonio up, they were going
on an excursion to an animal rescue centre, deep in
the rainforest. It would be a pleasant diversion from
worrying about his new school.

   Antonio had seen programmes about the rainforest
on television but nothing had prepared him for the
explosion of colour and the collision of noise and heat.
At the animal rescue centre, he fed the animals in the
enclosure, played with a baby monkey and saw a real,
live crocodile! Antonio thought about his life back in
England. It seemed rather safe and boring now. He
knew his mum was right – it was going to be a brilliant
adventure.

A confu<u>sion</u> of spellings

Write the missing word in each phrase. Use the word or letter clue to help you work out what the word is.

1.  an _____ of fizz   (explode)

2.  a long and boring _____ (divert)

3.  a dreadful _____   (confuse)

4.  an irritating _____ (invade)

5.  a happy _____   (conclude)

6. a clever i_____

7.  a funny t_____ show

8.  an important o_____

Ser<u>ious</u> spellings

Choose one of the adjectives from the box to describe each item. Cross out **a** or **an** to go with the adjective you choose.

Note: There are more adjectives than you need.

famous anxious dangerous enormous fabulous jealous mysterious glamorous delicious curious generous adventurous nervous venomous furious hazardous

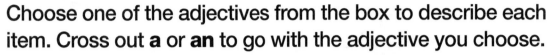

1. a / an _____ dinner

2. a / an _____ girl

3. a / an _____ boy

4. a / an _____ present

5. a / an _____ snake

6. a / an _____ road

7. a / an _____ wait

8. a / an _____ film star

Marvell<u>ous</u> –<u>ous</u> words

Can you remember these spellings?

Read each word out loud.

Circle any letters you think might cause you problems.

Cover up the word and then try to write it correctly.

Check, cover and write it again.

Read the word	Write the word	Write the word again
furious		
marvellous		
anxious		
glorious		
dangerous		
hazardous		
disastrous		
ridiculous		
suspicious		
poisonous		
ambitious		
numerous		
glamorous		
nervous		
mysterious		
enormous		

/shun/ collec<u>tion</u>s

Sort these words into the correct column.

What do you know about the words that end **–cian**?

Which column has the most words?

action	permission	electrician	attention	mathematician
physician	extension	passion	percussion	mansion
possession	politician	collection	technician	direction
obsession	beautician	education	discussion	musician
information	expansion	introduction	version	admission
competition	mention	optician	tension	impression

spelt **–tion**	spelt **–sion**	spelt **–ssion**	spelt **–cian**

Your mi<u>ss</u>ion: Learn these spellings

Add the /shun/ ending to these words.

Remember, you might need to change the root word.

Say the new word out loud to yourself before you write it.

associate _____

mathematics _____

attend _____

music _____

extend _____

express _____

educate _____

physics _____

compete _____

admit _____

invent _____

permit _____

impress _____

oppose _____

politics _____

electric _____

inject _____

obsess _____

expand _____

permit _____

submit _____

Spellings to make your head a<u>ch</u>e

Look at these words. Colour in all the words with the **/k/** sound spelt **ch**.

school	reach	headache	bunch	cheers
marcher	scheme	chicken	orchestra	punch
touch	bleach	chemistry	watch	searching
teach	preacher	echo	flinch	anchor
richer	chorus	chalk	chip	munching
mechanic	choice	cheese	character	each
crunching	champ	searcher	pinches	choir
chaos	archer	ache	which	punched
much	stomach	match	chasm	chunk

A s<u>ch</u>ooling in /k/ spelt <u>ch</u>

Look at the picture clue and write the missing word.

Each missing word uses the letters **ch** for the **/k/** sound.

1.	**2.**
3.	**4.**
5.	**6.**
7.	**8.**
9.	**10.**
11.	**12.**

1. Haul the _____ !

2. Hear the _____ sing.

3. Listen to the _____ .

4. Ouch! I have a terrible _____.

5. We have another day at _____.

6. This is a deep, dark _____.

7. Bats use _____ to navigate.

8. I am a _____. I fix cars.

9. Alice is the main _____ of Alice in Wonderland.

10. I am a _____. I do _____.

11. This villainous ch _____ has a wicked s _____.

12. I have a s _____ a _____.

/sh/ spelt <u>ch</u> letter match

Play this game with four players plus someone to draw the letters out of the bag. Cut out the words and give two words (one from the first row and one from the second row) to each player. Cut out the letters at the bottom of the page and put them in a bag. Ask someone to take out the letters one at a time and to read them out.

The players mark off the letters in their words. The winner is the first person to cross off all the letters in both their words.

s <u>a</u> <u>c</u> h e t	<u>c</u> h <u>e</u> f	q <u>u</u> <u>i</u> <u>c</u> h <u>e</u>	<u>c</u> h <u>a</u> l <u>e</u> t
<u>m</u> <u>o</u> <u>u</u> <u>s</u> <u>t</u> <u>a</u> <u>c</u> h <u>e</u>	<u>b</u> <u>r</u> <u>o</u> <u>c</u> h <u>u</u> <u>r</u> <u>e</u>	<u>m</u> <u>a</u> <u>c</u> h <u>i</u> <u>n</u> <u>e</u>	<u>p</u> <u>a</u> <u>r</u> <u>a</u> <u>c</u> h <u>u</u> <u>t</u> <u>e</u>

a	b	c	e	f	h	i	l	m
n	o	p	q	r	s	t	u	

A ni<u>ch</u>e spelling pattern

You will need yellow, blue and green colouring pencils or highlighters.

Race against your partner to colour in all the words.

- Colour the words where **ch** stands for **/k/** yellow.
- Colour the words where **ch** stands for **/sh/** blue.
- Colour the words where **ch** stands for **/ch/** green.

On your marks … get set … Go!

school	chef	headache	chalet	cheers
chateau	scheme	chicken	orchestra	machine
touch	bleach	chemistry	watch	searching
chaotic	charade	echo	parachute	anchor
niche	chorus	chalk	chip	pistachio
mechanic	sachet	cheese	character	each
crunching	champion	chute	pinches	choir
chaos	archer	ache	moustache	punched
quiche	stomach	match	chasm	chandelier

Conquer these grotesque spellings

Choose the correct spellings. Read each word carefully and decide which one is right. Cross out the wrong word. Remember, **–gue** spells /g/ and **–que** spells /k/. But, watch out, there is one pair of words where both are right.

conguered	conquered
catalogue	cataloque
unigue	unique
rogue	roque
grotesgue	grotesque
league	leaque
plague	plaque
opague	opaque
meringue	merinque
vague	vaque
intrigue	intrique
dialogue	dialoque
tongue	tonque
antigue	antique
technigue	technique

A crossword of intrigue

Solve the clues to complete the crossword. All the answers end either **–gue** or **–que**.

Across

(Hint: All these words end **–gue**)

3. Not very clear or well defined

4. Conversation in a story

6. The muscle in your mouth

9. To interest or fascinate

10. A group of sports teams competing against each other

Down

(Hint: All these words end **–que**)

1. The opposite of see-through

2. A metal sign in remembrance of a person or event

5. Extremely ugly, hideous

7. Old and valuable jewellery or furniture

8. Only one of its kind

Fa<u>sc</u>inating <u>s</u>pelling<u>s</u>

Sort these words into the correct column of the table.

Some words will need to be written in more than one column.

scent snow crescent creases lost fascinating silent lace scissors bossy city princess bicycle pencil scene centre fussy fancy books pasta pressed festival sentence muscles

/s/ spelt **ss**	/s/ spelt **c**	/s/ spelt **s**	/s/ spelt **sc**

Scenic spellings

Read the words at the bottom of the page, then fold them under to hide them. Use the words to complete the sentences.

1. Mia used _____ to cut out her picture.

2. The garden was full of the _____ of jasmine flowers.

3. Biology, chemistry and physics are all _____.

4. I think the history of England is _____.

5. The moon was a silver _____ in the starry sky.

6. The hikers' _____ down the mountain was slippery in the ice.

7. Bodybuilders lift heavy weights to build their _____.

8. We drove the _____ route along the coast.

- -

scissors	scent	scenic	crescent	muscles
	descent	fascinating	science	

/ay/ homophones

Cut out these word cards. Make pairs of the words that sound the same.

Muddle up the cards and turn them face down. Play a game of 'Pairs' with a partner. A pair is two words that sound the same but are spelt differently.

ate	prey	slay	way
sheikh	weight	rain	sleigh
veil	vein	eight	shake
vain	pray	reign	vale
weigh	wait	neigh	nay

Ob<u>ey</u> the spelling rules

Choose **ei**, **eigh** or **ey** for the spelling of the long /ay/ sound in these words.

1. The Queen of the North travelled in her sl_____ across the snow.

2. Please can you w_____ the flour for the pancakes?

3. My little sister has _____teen teddy bears.

4. We went next door to ask our n_____bour for our ball back.

5. We filled in a surv_____ about our favourite foods.

6. Our school uniform colours are gr_____ and yellow.

7. The boys wore harnesses to abs_____l down the tower.

8. The hawk could see its pr_____ in the field below.

9. The bride wore a pretty v_____l over her face.

10. The car drivers must ob_____ the traffic signals.

Today's challenge

Is the underlined word in each sentence singular or plural?
Write the answer.

1. Next <u>Thursday's</u> lunch will be roast chicken. _____

2. All the <u>cars'</u> windows are covered in ice. _____

3. The <u>girl's</u> bag is pink! _____

4. The <u>girls'</u> bags are pink! _____

5. Wait for <u>Mrs Parker's</u> signal. _____

Add the missing apostrophe to the correct place in each sentence.
Check the hints for help deciding if the noun you'll add an apostrophe
to is singular or plural.

1. The trousers legs are too long.

(Hint: The legs of the **trousers** are too long.)

2. The fishes scales sparkled.

(Hint: The scales of the **fishes** sparkled.)

3. The trees leaves turned a deep orange.

(Hint: The leaves of the **tree** turned a deep orange.)

4. The twins birthday is a day after mine.

(Hint: The birthday of the **twins** is the day after mine.)

5. Todays soup is carrot and coriander.

(Hint: The soup of **today** is carrot and coriander.)

Plural nouns and possessive apostrophes

Add the missing apostrophe to each of these phrases.

1. This weeks work

2. The next two weeks work

3. Nialls lunch

4. The boys lunches
   (**boys** plural)

5. The cars headlights
   (**car** singular)

6. The cars headlights
   (**cars** plural)

7. My sisters friend
   (**sister** singular)

8. My sisters friends
   (**sisters** plural)

9. The snakes venom
   (**snake** singular)

10. The snakes venom
    (**snake** plural)

11. The days activities
    (**day** singular)

12. The days activities
    (**days** plural)

13. Our fathers job
    (**father** singular)

14. Our fathers jobs
    (**father** plural)

15. The childs progress

16. The childrens progress

<u>Whose</u> pairs?

Cut out the word cards. Match up words that sound the same.

Cut out the definition cards. Match the words to the definitions.

Muddle up all the cards and place them face down. Play a game of 'Pairs' where a pair is a word and its definition.

bury	medal	berry	except
accept	whose	effect	meddle
weather	affect	who's	whether
cover completely	metal disk	small fruit	not including
consent to	of whom	result	interfere
climate	influence	who is	if

Whether to use 'weather' or 'whether'

Use the words in the box to complete the sentences.

You won't need to use every word.

buries	berries	accept	except	medal	meddle	who's
	whose	affect	effect	weather	whether	

1. The gold _____ was awarded to Mo Farah.

2. I don't know why you can't just _____ that I'm right!

3. The girls made a delicious smoothie with apples and _____.

4. Everyone has been invited to the party _____ me.

5. It doesn't matter _____ fault it is – just clear it up!

6. I don't know _____ they are coming or not.

7. Moira's frequent hiccups _____ our concentration for the worse.

8. The artist created an interesting _____ with oil and water.

9. _____ having hot dinners today?

10. Please don't _____ with the papers I've left on the table.

Throw <u>here</u>, <u>not</u> there!

Take a counter and throw it on the chart.

If you land on a word, say what the word means.

If you land on a definition, spell the word.

Tick off the squares as you land on them. Carry on until you have landed on each square.

forms a negative	here	shred	great
groan	back of a foot	not	tangle
hear	grate	recover	became bigger
grown	detect sound	heel	knot
this place	heal	wonderful	moan

Great spelling practice!

Use the words in the box to complete the sentences.

hear   here   grate   great   not   knot   grown
groan   heels   heals   he'll

1. Don't let Ben climb the wall, _____ fall and hurt himself.

2. "Speak up!" said Grandpa. "I can't _____ you when you mumble!"

3. Kat and Dan grumble and _____ when Mum serves fish pie.

4. What time will your friends get _____ ?

5. No, that's _____ the answer.

6. Lauren will _____ the cheese for dinner.

7. Well done, Caitlin, that was _____ !

8. My brother has _____ taller than my mother.

9. We cannot go swimming until my grazed knee _____ .

10. Stand with your _____ together and your toes apart.

11. We learned to tie a slip _____ at summer camp.

Play <u>fair</u>

Take a counter and throw it on the chart.

If you land on a word, say what the word means.

If you land on a definition, spell the word.

Tick off the squares as you land on them. Carry on until you have landed on each square.

meet	aircraft	plane	long hair
animal flesh	fair	mane	piece
fare	light fog	encounter	meat
calmness	plain	part of something	light or pleasant
failed to catch	most important	missed	peace
main	mist	cost of travel	obvious or basic

Have you missed these homophones?

Use the words in the box to complete the sentences.

You will not need to use all the words.

mist   missed   mane   main   plane   plain

peace   piece   meet   meat   fair   fare

1.   The zebras on the _____ suddenly smelled a lion.

2.   Jane flew in a _____ to her holiday in Spain.

3.   Daniel is the _____ character in our play.

4.   Curtsey and smile when you _____ the Queen.

5.   The autumn _____ made our hair damp.

6.   The girls at the stables brushed the pony's _____ .

7.   We couldn't afford the bus _____ so we walked home.

8.   We ran as fast as we could, but we still _____ the train.

9.   Dad took us to the _____ on Saturday to go on the rides.

10. Milly fell flat on her face and chipped a small _____ off her tooth.

Win the game: <u>reign</u> supreme!

Take a counter and throw it on the chart.

If you land on a word, say what the word means.

If you land on a definition, spell the word.

Tick off the squares as you land on them. The first person to land on each square is the winner.

not female	stop mechanically	past of 'see'	rain
break	post	bawl	seen
scene	rule	mail	water from the sky
straps to control horses	reign	site or location	cry or shout
brake	fall apart or stop working	male	rein

Homophones to make you <u>bawl</u>

Use the words in the box to complete the sentences.
You won't need to use all the words.

ball bawled male mail brake break
rain rein reign seen scene

1. Have you _____ who's coming down road!

2. Don't forget to _____ before you drive around the corner.

3. Practise for ten more minutes, then we'll take a _____ .

4. We have a new _____ teacher for modern dance.

5. The first _____ of the film takes place ten years earlier.

6. Camping in the _____ is not much fun.

7. The cricket _____ flew through the air and hit the window.

8. The jockey held on tightly to the _____ .

9. Trish sat on the floor and _____ her eyes out.